CALCUTTA NIGHTS

HEMENDRA KUMAR ROY

Translated by Rajat Chaudhuri

PAPER
MISSILE

NIYOGI
BOOKS

Raater Kolkata (*Calcutta Nights*) by Hemendra Kumar Roy, writing under the nom de plume of Meghnad Gupta, was first published by Pratik, Kolkata (1923)

Published by
NIYOGI BOOKS
Block D, Building No. 77,
Okhla Industrial Area, Phase-I,
New Delhi-110 020, INDIA
Tel: 91-11-26816301, 26818960
Email: niyogibooks@gmail.com
Website: www.niyogibooksindia.com

Original Bengali text © Sudeshna Chakraborti
Translation © Rajat Chaudhuri

Editor: Mohua Mitra
Design: Shashi Bhushan Prasad
Cover Design: Pinaki De

ISBN: 978-93-89136-45-6
Publication: 2020

Printed at: Niyogi Offset Pvt. Ltd., New Delhi, India

CONTENTS

A young Hemendra Kumar Roy with his wife Renuka
Courtesy: The Roy family archives

PREFACE: NIGHTS IN THE CITY

A hundred years ago, a young man roamed the mean streets of Calcutta—the capital of British India, night after night, alone and almost unarmed. From the Chitpur bordellos to the Chinese gambling dens of Territi Bazaar, from the green rooms of Bengali theatres to the hideouts of ruthless hoodlums of Mechhobazaar and beyond. Who was this Meghnad Gupta, who was scouring the wastelands of a metropolis while war raged the world over, and the country was ripe for change? Who was this Meghnad Gupta who quotes Tagore at the drop of a hat just as easily as he narrates scenes from the inner recesses of Calcutta's houses of ill repute where babus cavorted with nautch girls? Do we know him? Perhaps we do …

Calcutta Nights is the real-life story and memoir of this enigmatic Meghnad Gupta who, as the reader will soon discover, is one of the pioneering creators of Bengali fiction—Hemendra Kumar Roy. Translated into English almost a century after the first publication of *Raater Kolkata* in 1923, the popular author of detective novels, sci-fi and children's books reveals the darkest secrets of the second city of the erstwhile British Empire.

Raater Kolkata (*Calcutta Nights*), as someone has said, is the *Hootum Pyanchar Naksha* (*The Observant Owl: Hootum's Vignettes of Nineteenth-century Calcutta*) of the early twentieth century.

AN INTRODUCTION TO BABUS, BORDELLOS, AND GASLIT NIGHTS

Calcutta Nights was written almost a hundred years ago and first published in Bengali as *Raater Kolkata* (author Meghnad Gupta) in 1923. Much of this book is set in a time which stretches back even further to the first two decades of the twentieth century. Calcutta was still the capital of British ruled India then—a bustling metropolis with a dark underbelly, where untold dangers lurked behind the glamour and shine.

Armed with just a stout stick, the celebrated author and crime fiction writer Hemendra Kumar Roy, who used the pseudonym 'Meghnad Gupta' for this work, roamed about in the darkness of Calcutta's mean streets, alone every night. Not to indulge and drown in its sins but to experience, learn and tell true stories.

The first two decades of the last century, which is the backdrop for this book, were turbulent times for this country in general and Bengal in particular. The first Partition of Bengal happened in 1905 with Curzon as Viceroy, the Alipore Bomb Case trials commenced near the end of that decade, and the capital of India was shifted from Calcutta to Delhi in 1911. Following the partition of 1905, there was severe criticism of the British 'divide and rule' policy because it had driven a wedge between the largely Muslim-majority-eastern from the largely Hindu-majority-western part of Bengal. With increased civil unrest and violence, the decision to partition Bengal was reversed by the British in 1911. Then in 1912 the provinces of Bihar and Orissa were carved out of Bengal Presidency. The second decade of the 1900s also saw the emergence of Gandhi's leadership and the launching of his Non-Cooperation

Movement. In this decade too, Rabindranath Tagore was awarded the Nobel prize for literature while the first commercial aircraft flew in this country. The First World War was also fought in this eventful second decade of the twentieth century.

No doubt, the years in which this book is set were interesting times. Written in an age very different from ours, some views of the author could be jarring for our neurotic and politically-correct present. However, any such view needs to be tempered by the understanding of the socio-political contexts as well as the distance of a century that separates us from Meghnad Gupta's Calcutta, the second city of the erstwhile British Empire.

I was made aware of the Bangla original *Raater Kolkata* (*Calcutta Nights*) quite accidentally at an adda session with friends at the old-world Broadway bar in central Calcutta which is one of the areas the author must have passed through during his nocturnal wanderings. The book was first published in 1923, but luckily Urbi Prakasan had reprinted it a few years ago, which is why I could quickly get hold of a copy. I read it rapt over the period of a weekend, realising that this is an important social and historical document about the city in the tradition of works like *Kalikata Kamalalay* (1823) and *Nabababubilas* (1825) by Bhabani Charan Bandopadhyay, *Alaaler Ghore Dulaal* (1858) by Parichand Mitra, *Sachitra Guljarnagar* (1871) a satirical novel by Kedaranatha Datta, and of course Kaliprasanna Sinha's *Hootum Pyanchar Naksha* (Hootum's Sketches of Nineteenth Century Calcutta, 1862), which book the author mentions in his prologue.

Hootum's work and some of the others mentioned above are *naksha*s or sketches, a form popular in those times and in fact our book, though written at least half a century later, has the characteristics of a 'sketch'. Arun Nag, referring to Jatindramohan Ghosh's essay about the subject, points out in his annotated *Hootum Pyanchar Naksha* (2018), that a sketch is characterised by the presence of humour, social satire, a tendency towards brevity, instructions to remove social evils, exaggeration, unrefined language, and suggestive descriptions among other things. Besides all these, *Calcutta Nights* also shares some similarities of character with books like *Crime and Religious Beliefs in India* by Augustus Somerville. So it did not take me long to decide to translate this book into English as I felt this should reach a wider audience.

For Calcutta-lovers, adventure enthusiasts, criminologists, history buffs, researchers, and readers of all stripes and colours, this little book is a veritable goldmine. Like a festive Bengali meal albeit peppered with darkness, this book offers an extended spread in bite-sized portions. Those interested to know more about the debauchery of the *hothath-babus*, the stories of ruthless goons with great musical talent, the glamour of European women of the night in Eden Gardens, the mystery phaeton cars plying around Chowringhee, the dance of lady luck in Chinese gambling dens, the backstage intrigues of Bengali playhouses, the darkness of beggars' hovels, or the scent of jasmine in the hair buns of verandah-belles will find something in these pages.

While translating this book, I have tried to retain some Bengali words and sometimes employed archaic expressions or slightly convoluted constructions to best reproduce the language and mood of those times. For the benefit of the interested reader and researcher alike, I have also added detailed endnotes to further illuminate the setting of this book while including suggestions for further reading.

A simplified romanisation has been used for place names approximating the Bengali pronunciation, exceptions being Calcutta, Chowringhee and a few others. Words in Bengali which won't be familiar to all readers have been italicised in their first use. Also, it won't be out of place to mention here that Anindita Roy Chowdhury in her meticulously researched *Prostitution in Calcutta during the Twentieth Century—A Study in Gender Perspective* had included translated passages from one chapter of *Raater Kolkata*. These translated passages sourced from Biswanath Joardar's *Prostitution in Nineteenth and Early Twentieth Century Calcutta* have helped me a couple of times to take decisions about the choice of certain words in that chapter.

Hemendra Kumar Roy was undoubtedly an accomplished stylist and in my translation of his work, I have tried my best to retain the flavour of the original. In my own reading of this little dynamite of a volume, I have encountered Dickensian darkness under the gaslights of Calcutta's streets, I have enjoyed gothic interludes in scenes of winter nights that would remind you of Edgar Allan Poe and I have also sensed a writer's keen interest in backstory and character. Being a writer myself, this aspect of *Calcutta Nights*, which is essentially a memoir infused with social satire, adventure and insights about a place, a time, and a people, appealed to my sensibilities. I hope the reader will enjoy the nuances of his style in this translation as we do in the original.

In a few rare instances certain expressions, words, slants have been removed or expressed differently in this translated text to address the genuine sensitivities of our times. This has been done only two or three times in the whole book without affecting the spirit of the narrative.

While there is no indication in the 1923 edition of *Raater Kolkata* that the author was using a pseudonym, the third Urbi edition (January, 2018) tells us that the author of *Calcutta Nights* was no one else but the popular Bengali writer Hemendra Kumar Roy (1888-1963). This is supported with a quote from a feature by Satadal Goswami, which appeared in *Desh* magazine (15 October, 1988), who asserts that Hemendra Kumar Roy wrote this book with the pseudonym Meghnad Gupta. He goes on to say that Roy used an assumed name because he didn't want his guardians to find out that he had written this book. There is other evidence presented in the Urbi volume proving that Hemendra Kumar Roy, the much-loved author of detective fiction, children's literature, and science fiction, indeed wrote *Calcutta Nights*. Now we also know the real identity of the author from authoritative sources like his family members.

I feel honoured to be able to present Hemendra Kumar Roy's portrait of my city to a wider audience. My efforts wouldn't have gone in vain if it created further interest about the past, present and future of Calcutta.

Rajat Chaudhuri
Kolkata

PROLOGUE

Calcutta Nights has been written for an adult male audience.

In *Hootum Pyanchar Naksha* (*Hootum's Vignettes of Nineteenth-century Calcutta*), we get a picture of the Calcutta of those times. My book too is a series of sketches or *naksha*. Here you will find images from certain time periods of the Calcutta of modern times. But my brush doesn't have the wide and mature palette that Hootum possessed, it's quite possible people won't like it. I am only banking on the fact that if milk isn't readily available, people will happily drink *ghol*, the bland 'buttermilk' made by churning out the creamy 'butter' from the milk.

If nothing else, these vignettes will be perfect medicine for many whose vision has been clouded by cataract. For most of us, the mysteries of Calcutta's nights are exceedingly blurred. *Calcutta Nights* will cleanse their vision. Fathers of young boys and girls will realise where and what the real dangers are. It is because of their carelessness that minors fall into bad company, and begin their visits to hell.

Still, I haven't provided a complete picture. I could have drawn the whole picture, but that completeness is so unimaginably fearsome that I didn't feel like attempting it. The little I have presented might indeed raise the hackles of champions of morality. But what can I do, there is no way one can camouflage this. 'Sketches' of this nature cannot be written in a more courteous style and in a more decent language. But I have been more careful than Hootum both in the matter of language and subject. To depict local colour, I have occasionally taken recourse to the use of words from rural dialect and have at times raised the curtains to hell. In certain instances, I haven't been able to completely avoid *adirasa* or eroticism. However, such dialect words, scenes from hell, and eroticism are very much present in the highbrow literature of these times. Moreover, modern novelists have progressed further than I have. My only consolation is in the fact that compared to modern novels and plays, *Calcutta Nights* is sacred like the Bible. The diligent reader will also notice that I have always depicted sin for what it is. I have tried to evoke hate and displeasure towards it and, unlike many modern novels, nowhere in this book is there an attempt to evoke sympathy for sin in the reader's mind. So I am firm in my belief that not a single reader will find *Calcutta Nights* to be obscene. There is no effort in this book to unfairly present obscenities.

I have been witness to most of the things mentioned and written here. I could have written about many other things if I had depended on hearsay, but I didn't do that. Like a detective, I have roamed the streets to gather these accounts. While gathering the accounts of the prostitutes' quarters, I have received assistance from many first rate 'experts'. If there is any such expert among the readers, he can verify whether the material obtained from my own 'experts' are dependable or not. I am still left with an uncounted store of material which covers many other facets of Calcutta. If the response from the reading public is one of eagerness, then I will be back with those in the near future. Otherwise, this will be the end of it.

Meghnad Gupta
(Hemendra Kumar Roy)

SCENE ONE
EVERYDAY PICTURE OF THE CITY

Calcutta.

Second city of the British empire, India's most important urban centre, Paris of the East, melting pot of all races, pride of Bengalis, cradle of the renaissance, city of palaces!

Day and night, multitudes pass through the streets—flowing like a stream. Alongside ancient palanquins from mythical king Mandhata's times, bullock-carts and pedestrians, run ultra-modern electric trams, buses and motorcars while aircrafts fly above, casting shadows on her expanse. Spectacles dangling on their noses, shod in fancy shoes and with fashionable hairstyles, the cane-wielding *kapure-babus*—the upper class gentlemen with social capital and recognition only on the outside; impeccably attired in western clothes over their swarthy forms; the great specimens of *ingo-bongos* or the anglophile Bengalis; donning curious hats and a variety of dresses the Parsis, Gujeratis, Marathis, Sikhs, Pathans, Kabulis, Nepalis, Bhutanese, Punjabis, Mongols, Japanese, Chinese and Marwaris among a variety of human specimens from the entire East; English, Scotch, Irish, French and Americans among aggressive specimens of western races, and alongside these, half-naked Oriyas, and completely naked groups of Naga mendicants ... such a curious kedgeree of humanity is not to be found anywhere in the world. At one side colourful mansions reach out to the sky, and in their shadows lean mud walls of cottages plastered with dung cakes—a rare sight anywhere else. On one flank of the street, like wealth personified, are well-dressed, nonchalant, vehicle-riders, blessed sons of Lakshmi—the Goddess of Wealth—ignorant to the sorrows and scarcities of the world, and on the other side, right there in the dust of the street, lying on blankets riddled with holes, worshippers of permanent destitution, hooded-eyed, skin-and-bones bands of poor beggars, gasping their last and waiting for death. And right in front of their drooping eyelids, beating huge drums—the *dhaak*s and dhols—and blowing trumpets, wafting flowery perfumes, their kilted scarves and drapes billowing, pass bands of the groom's party of a marriage ceremony. Where else can one see such a crooked smile on the lips of destiny? Life and death live here together, like thorn and blossom on the same branch.

It was about Calcutta that acclaimed poet Satyendranath Dutta said—

> *Ei Kolikata—Kalikakhsetra, kahini ihar sobar sruto,*
> *Bishnu chakra ghurechhe hethae, Mahesher padodhule e puto*
> *Hindur kali achhen hethae, Musalmaner Moula Ali,*
> *Chari koney sadhu pir charijon muskil asan cherag jali*
> *Sakal dharma milechhe hethae samanyaer mantra-surey*
> *Swagata sadhak-bhakta-brinda marater Baikunthapurey*

Roughly translated it reads:

'This Kolkata—Kalika's ground, everyone has heard its story,
Bishnu's discus spun here—Mahesh's feet made it holy

Here's the abode of the Hindus' Kali, and Maula Ali of
the Musalman,
Four pirs and sadhus at four corners, light the lamp
of redemption,
All religions have merged here, in a tune of hymn and harmony
This earthly paradise welcomes, every worshipper and devotee.'

And truly Calcutta on first acquaintance looks like a city which
is a pilgrimage for sadhus, a place for religious practice of
devotees, and an abode of the sacred. Hindu temples of Kali,
Tara, Mahadev, Sani, Jagaddhatri, Sitala, Buddhist viharas, Jain
shrines of Pareshnath, Christian churches, mosques of Muslims
are scattered all over—holding their heads up against the smoke
swathed sky—a diversity of styles of different ideologies. At every
step, a temple or the other with their crowds of devotees draws the
attention of pedestrians. Scenes of religious rituals and routine
prayers being offered morning and evening abound, amidst the
blowing of conches, the clamour of visitors. By observing the
polished floors, the bright gold ornaments of the deities, and
the softness and signs of indulgence in the bearings of temple
attendants, it does not take time to realise that most of the Hindu
gods and goddesses are well-off.

But without a sharp eye, no one would be able to decipher the
extent of wrongs, the extent of vileness and brutality concealed
beneath this outward shield of religiosity. Despite Chitteswari
of Chitpur at one end and Kalikadebi of Kalighat at the other
keeping watch on the domain of Calcutta, every day Satan and
his sinful followers enter the city in hordes, pulling wool over
their divine eyes.

Poet Satyendranath says—

Ei Kolikata byagrhobahini chhilo he ekoda bagher basa
Bagher moton manush jahara tahaderi chhilo jawa o asha!

('This Kolkata on a tiger rides, 'twas once a tiger's den
Those men who were tiger-like, would come and go often!')

Just as in those times there were people who were like tigers,
this day too there is no dearth of tigers in human garb in
Calcutta. Rather the legions of these tiger-people have grown.
But they are more tiger-like in their cruelty and beastliness
rather than in vigour and energy. These tigers and tigresses are
scattered all across the city—through the day they move about
in groups amongst us. Always alert and waiting for prey, like an
invisible pestilence. We don't know them, but they have every
bit of information about us at their fingertips. When at night the
curtain of deepest darkness descends on the heart of Calcutta,
these tigers and tigresses employing trickery, attack us unawares.
Tigers of the wild crave human flesh, but these human tigers
want the substance of our souls. And once someone's soul comes
into their clutches, he cannot be saved. Easy-going parents from
villages, you send your naive children to Calcutta to become
worthy humans. But often, under the influence of these tigers
and tigresses, their humanity is drained and they return home
transformed into a beast or a ghost.

No one should be fooled by the outward sheen, the glamorous
beauty, the light and laughter, the mock-religiosity, the crowds
at temples, churches and mosques of Calcutta. How much
darkness has congealed at the lamp's base—today we will reveal

some of those secret scenes. We spend our lives cradled by this Calcutta; our lives, our deaths, our marriages are in sync with the rhythms of this Calcutta, our hearts are full with pride and we feel honoured being residents of Calcutta. Yet how many among us have seen the true face of Calcutta? How many of us dare to roam about in the silence of the deepest night amongst Calcutta's scary and impassable forest of palaces? How many are interested to know about the romances unfolding, the fascinating incidents, the tragedies being played out around us each day? What is the value of a report in the morning newspaper? Braving great dangers, time and again avoiding the knives of hoodlums, in the spirit of adventure, I alone, like a creature of darkness, just a short and stout stick on my person, have regularly roamed the streets of Calcutta from evening till the end of night. Without bothering about moral corruption, I have entered evil and forbidden places with no hesitation. My long experience cannot fit into these pages. Here I will provide some glimpses, some hints. If readers enjoy, then in future I will try to describe different facets of Calcutta in greater detail.

SCENE TWO
CALCUTTA STREETS

The shadows of evening fall slowly across the dusty, smoke-swathed face of Calcutta.

The real life of Calcutta begins now. During the day it is hard to spy anything with the slightest hint of mystery in the urban jungle of Calcutta, amidst the hubbub of business, and in the comings and goings of clerks. Evening ushers in the mysteries—especially Saturday evenings. Gas lamps light up every street, flocks of owls flutter away overhead etching inky-black marks across the grim sky, and from the darkness at the bends and corners of alleyways, swarthy ugly faces begin to peep and snoop. Now it's time for the saint's rest and the hour for Satan's wakefulness.

Now the tired and weary faces of clerks can no more be seen on the streets, and the very streets which in daytime hum and throb with the sounds of vehicles and pedestrians, lie still and deserted. If you venture into Clive Street, Strand Road, the roads adjoining the High Court or the neighbourhoods of Radhabazaar and Murgihata after nine in the evening, you will be struck by an abnormal stillness. Still later in the night, you get a creepy feeling walking these neighbourhoods and are startled by your own footsteps. There is no one around, and the only presences are the silence and darkness. As if these roads are haunted—as if the mysteries of the netherworld are congealed around them.

But the northern stretch of Chitpur Road hasn't fallen asleep, though its appearance has been transformed—the pedestrians there no more look busy, work-weary or dirty. One can see they are out looking for leisure and enjoyment. Watching them no one will vouch for the fact that these are the same people who during the day, wearing dirty sweat-soaked clothes, their bellies stuffed with parboiled rice and vegetables, had run breathless like horses of hackney-carriages towards their offices and there, having pen-pushed through the day, had stomached the raps of the *barobabu*—the head clerk—and the threats of the saheb, before going homewards, puffing and panting. Tomorrow is Sunday, no morning rush to reach office, so everyone's face is aglow with untrammeled happiness! Shiny hair clipped short or kept long and fashionably coiffed, faces fresh and glowing from the application of Hazeline snow, some with stylish eyeglasses, cheap cigarettes dangling from their lips, donning churidar-punjabis of a fine fabric, wearing a fine, pleated homemade handloom cloth, wristwatch on the left hand and silver encased cane in the right, rings on their fingers and fancy shoes of different shapes and sizes on their feet. Some have stuffed their pockets with money, and the scent of this silver has attracted some carefree fair-weather friends. At the crossing of Beadon Square, the leaders of these groups buy strings of jasmine. One is immediately taken out and twined around the wrist—the rest in time will adorn the hair of some courtesan—a 'verandah-belle'. The babus hurry on while casting shameless and thirsty eyes at the verandahs on both sides. The clock will strike eight anytime now; by that hour one has to acquire the goddess of spirits from Mama's booze shop. Probably these Abu Hussains in a single day will squander away a month's hard-earned income in the streams of pleasure. When at night's end or at dawn the next day, lolling with fatigue, eyes bloodshot from lack of sleep and intoxication, they return home panting, then if one went through their pockets, they wouldn't be able to find half a rupee on them.

A stream of vehicles drive down the street—tomtom, landau, phaeton, *palki-gari*, motorbus and mostly 'taxi'! In some of these, fair-skinned donkeys sit completely unconcerned about the world, their expression seems to convey their belief that there is no one human enough in this world other than them, those who are walking down the street are no better than worms and insects and if they are crushed under the wheels, the world wouldn't have suffered the minutest loss. Having spent their day in stupor, these barn-owls of Lakshmi, wake up in the darkness of evening like the pipistrelle-bats and owls, and set out from home at night heading for their fixed and appointed pleasure dens. They are unable to get rid of the fatigue of their monotonous lives without a regular visit. Many of the riders are Marwaris. Reared on a diet of roasted gram flour or *chhatu*, in the dry western country, they first arrived with chattels on their heads and settled down in Bengal. Then during the last war, thanks to 'speculation' they found themselves suddenly overburdened with silver and gold. These days, they have become overly engaged in shedding some of this burden in haste. The luxury loving Bengalis and their much-adored city Calcutta is pre-eminent in the Orient for the latest fashion. Emulating the Bengali babus the Marwaris are also forgetting the taste of the roasted gram flour *chhatu* and shedding their rusticity for city-bred looks—broken Bangla words on their lips and dressed in Bengali clothes. Many have completely chopped off or reduced the length of their scalp lock—the small tuft of hair left long and loose at the back of their clean-shaven pate. They now sport a fashionable 'ten-anna-six-anna' hairstyle. Bengali Abu Husseans are embittered by their gall because all the pretty nymphs of the city are today attracted to the newly-arrived wealthy 'babus'. They are the nouveau riche, showering money at the drop of a hat—how could the Bengali babus possibly measure up to them?

Most of the *hotath-babu*s, the parvenus among babus, ride taxis. By helping themselves from the iron safes or jewel boxes of their parents, by executing 'hand-notes' or by some other means, they have suddenly obtained some money. Now they will make good use of it. In a few days their pockets will be empty like the Garher Maath—the open fields of Calcutta's esplanade. It might also be observed that having failed to pay the taxi fare, many of them with haggard faces are appearing as accused in court.

Most of the vehicles empty out near Sonagachhi and Rupagachhi. Among those alighting are not only the *hotath-babu*s and Marwaris; get a little closer and you will see many a famous judge, magistrate, barrister, lawyer, attorney, doctor, MLC, non-cooperator, speaker, learned editor, and litterateur in this group. In fact, I cannot falsely claim that some of those saintly gentlemen of upright character who are earning kudos for themselves by delivering lucid public speeches in support of evicting prostitutes from the city, are not among their ranks. During my nightly wanderings I have seen many heads of Hindu, Christian, Muslim and Brahmo communities in these places.

Initially I used to be surprised; I couldn't believe my eyes. Now with habit, I am no more surprised. Not because I have stopped trusting my eyesight, but because I have lost all faith in the so-called moral integrity of the people of Calcutta. But I don't want to record here who I have seen where and when. However I can say with confidence that most people of Calcutta irrespective of race or religion, pay visits to prostitutes' quarters. They are never exposed in society; their masks are so perfect.

As night deepens, and as every part of Calcutta falls silent, the exuberant cheer of Chitpur rises higher still. At this time one sees rows of taxis emerging from the side streets around the area and hurtling down Chitpur road towards the Maidan. Most of their passengers would be raving drunk by then, and almost in every vehicle there would be one or two women with strings of flowers in their tightly coiled buns, lying in the laps or on the chests of the gentlemen. Inside the car everyone would be shrieking with merriment, some declaring their love at the top of their voices, some singing raunchy songs, and some talking gibberish under the grip of intoxication. In some vehicles harmoniums would be played in accompaniment to songs which went like this—

Amar bhalobasha abar kothay basha bendheche
Piriter parota kheye motaa hoyeche
Maashe maashe baarche bhaaraa
Baariuli dichhe taaraa
Goylapaaraar moilaa chhoraa praane mereche!'

'Where has my love built its nest, again;
Fed on the fare of desire, it does fatten

The monthly rent is on the rise
The landlady's pokes and prods, likewise
But the swarthy lad from the milkmen's quarters—my heart he
has stolen!'

And there is no restraint even on kissing and hugging in open cars, right on the street and in full public view.

If during evening *arati*—the ritual waving of lights to greet the gods and goddesses—one happens to visit the temples of Kali and other deities on the streets of Calcutta, one would notice something quite interesting. Crowds of men and women are gathered in front of the temple. A few true devotees and women from poor but decent families are present no doubt, but a large number of the remaining are men on the prowl, women of loose morals from respectable households, and prostitutes. Some of these women from decent households may not have a guardian to take care of them, but for whatever reason they are unable to hawk their youth and beauty in public like the 'bazaar prostitutes' do. They come to these temples in the evening under the guise of viewing the idol. Like attracts like. The purpose of their visit is accomplished as soon as, from under their half-veils, they have exchanged meaningful glances with a man on the prowl. Then, when they set off for home, it is often found that there is no dearth of men following in their footsteps— like bees tempted by nectar. At times, under the grip of some illusion, even the best and seasoned hunters end up following chaste married women of socially respectable families. The result is a limping retreat after having tasted the bitter-pill of a lathi-wielding guard. But despite such disgrace, good sense doesn't prevail among these wretched people. Right the next day they are found waiting at the temple door at the right hour. There is a class of men who prefer these undercover women of loose morals, from socially respectable families, rather than 'common prostitutes'. Prostitutes also know the inclinations of this sort. So, many among them, with veils drawn like married women of common folk, visit the temple, and under the ruse of watching the evening *arati* don't let a chance pass to pull wool over the eyes of men. This habit of following women sometimes ends in the acting out of tragic-comic scenes. At times there is a gathering of more than one connoisseur of beauty around a single woman. Then each of them, trying to shake the other off, adopts assorted strategies—staring down, trading expletives, and fights—nothing is off-limits. The characters of dogs and cats still lie concealed in human nature.

In the early hours before dawn, a similar kind of scene unfolds near the banks of the Ganga. Under the cover of darkness of the predawn hours, many women from socially respectable families, who are wary of the lecherous looks of other men, cover their faces as they go for their morning dip. But they are not all devoted to their husbands like the legendary Sati Savitri. There is much impurity among their lot, and they don't miss making good use of this golden opportunity. Men on the prowl are also aware of this. They come out in groups during this time and lie in wait for the prey. Many of them know of empty houses. They take their captured prey to these houses. At times mild-mannered women of good character, falling into temptation, become instruments of their own ruin. A few never return home in their lifetime. Women from our homes, unaccompanied by a male escort, shouldn't be allowed to go for a bath in the Ganga in the early hours preceding dawn.

I have heard that on the banks of the Ganga, in the Barabazaar area, there are empty houses for women who hail from the western or north western part of the country or are of mixed breed. But I have never seen them with my own eyes. Men from other places are supposed to be collected and kept in these houses for these women. One hears that 'western' young women get their desire satiated by sleeping with these assorted men, and obviously they spend money for it. But depending on hearsay, I can't comment further. This can be true or false but there is nothing impossible in Calcutta.

I say nothing's impossible because I have come to know about an even more bizarre incident happening in a decent Bengali neighbourhood. The 'heroine' of this ugly romance is a woman from a rich and famous Calcutta family which has a long association with this city. Her husband passed away at a young age without leaving any guardian to look after the widowed wife. This woman used to live alone with her only male child in a huge mansion situated in some locality near the bank of the Ganga. The means she adopted to satiate her desire was as ugly as it was novel. In the early hours before dawn she, accompanied by a few trusted guards and doormen—the durwans of her home— would go for a bath in the Ganga. But she didn't take a bath. I have already mentioned that at this time a particular class of men also ventured out for prey. This glamorous lady would prey on these hunters! She would bring home someone who struck her fancy. Some of them on seeing the big car and the durwans would be apprehensive of going home with her and would be ready to

forsake the attraction of such glamour and make a hasty escape,
thinking perhaps that this is some wicked trap. But then too, the
seductive siren wouldn't let them go. At her signal the durwan
would pounce upon that coward lover, bundling him into the
car. When the car rolled through the gates of the huge mansion,
the poor prisoner, frozen with fear, would think that he would
definitely be kidnapped and murdered that day. There was a
time, when this woman looking for unknown lovers, would often
venture out on such wonderful trysts. Nowadays she has become
subdued because her son had come of age.

Ding, dong, ding! The clock strikes three. At this time most
of these babus, who are given to a fanciful profligate living, put
an end to their night's merrymaking and head home. The four
corners of Chitpur become animated with intermittent motor
horns. Many have given away their last penny as an offering to
the presiding goddess of the night and are left with no other
option this day but to depend on their two stout legs. With their
rumpled dresses stained by the crimson juice from chewing
paan—the betel-leaf—tousled hair, and bloodshot eyes from a
night of revelry and intoxication, the night birds return home,
banging repeatedly against gaslight posts. At street corners the
police guards dozing on the raised platforms supporting the front
steps of houses, hearing footsteps, suddenly spring up wide awake
and with a threatening 'Who goes there!' catch hold of them and
raining blows, drag them to the police station.

Where there are no such guards around, suddenly, as if
springing from the sky, some stout black, tall and well-built
figures appear! And then, before the drunkards are shocked out
of their intoxication, the strange figures grab and snatch their

shawls and silk scarves, watches, chains or whatever they can get and suddenly disappear just as they had appeared. Those who are brave enough to resist them are rewarded with the close acquaintance of a sharp and shiny six inches of steel. Those birds of the night who having avoided such dangers, finally manage to arrive at their abodes—where their devoted wives had soaked the bed with their tears all night—are really fortunate. For once do reflect as to what element they are made of—these people who, defying monetary losses, loss of health, raining insult and even threats to life, pursue this lifestyle.

At night the scene in the *firangi* neighbourhood—the European and Anglo-Indian settlement of Calcutta—is of a different nature. There the spectacle of life is visible in places like Chowringhee, Curzon Park, Eden Gardens, Garher Maath, and within the racing grounds. The main difference between this area and the Bengali neighbourhoods is that here, generally, there is no clamour or filthiness. Just as the people here are well dressed and attractive, the neighbourhood is likewise. Numerous shops and hotels around Chowringhee, wearing garlands of light, seem to be welcoming the passer-by. A look inside gives the impression that bits of sparkling fairyland by some quirk of fate have suddenly landed here. So much light! So many flowers, vines and leaves! Such decorations! The eyes get satiated. Honeyed voices weave a rhythmic harmony, and the beautiful people come and go—nowhere a jarring note, everything executed with clockwork precision. Bengalis do not know how to enjoy life in this manner.

Crowds teem in front of the glittering edifices housing bioscopes and theatre-halls that line the streets of this area. In these crowds one can see a grand mix of Bengalis, Marwaris,

Muslims and Europeans. At times, amongst the hordes of the dark-skinned—like blooming roses in a jungle of thorns—white women with their glowing beauty and dresses enchant the eyes and the mind. Young Bengali men, thirsting for such beauty, stand in groups in front of most of these playhouses. Motorcars arrive one after the other and from these, flocks of fair-skinned European beauties in colourful fashionable dresses alight and the young men stare at them with hopeless but thirsty eyes! But alas this is like, as the saying goes—oiling and sprucing the moustache in anticipation of tasting the jackfruit while it is still on the tree or in other words, counting the chickens before they are hatched. Poet Dwijendralal had unambiguously stated that it is not possible to 'devour' a blooming sixteen-year old girl only with one's eyes! And Rabindranath had expressed what's in the mind of these young men through these two lines of verse—

'Bidhi daagor aankhi jodi diyechhile
Shey ki, aamaar paane bhuley poribenaa!'"

'If God has bestowed you with such beautiful large eyes
Will those not unknowingly cast a look upon me!'

The evening dresses of modern European beauties are dangerous indeed. First of all their complexion is beautiful like the juicy pink seeds of cracked pomegranates, their youthful busts are exposed by deep necklines, and many of them, with the amazing bare beauty of their ample milk-white cleavages, completely freeze the viewer's eyes. Murderers kill the body but these fair beauties kill the minds of men. They should be punished according to law.

Young men beware, it is fruitless to cast a look upon these will-o'-
the-wisps of the *firangi* or European (as well as Eurasian or Anglo-
Indian) neighbourhood because they display but never submit.
A class of Bengali women also roams the streets in this crowd.
They are also grotesquely dressed—a hotch-potch of home and
European fashion. Still many I suppose lament and wonder why
these women haven't yet learnt to venture out in clothes revealing
bare bosoms. We believe that in the near future, very probably,
there will be no more occasion to lament upon this—'that day
will come soon, no doubt it will!'

In the evening a particular kind of phaeton drives around
the streets of this area, interestingly enough, without a single
passenger. The groom, coachman, the horses, and the size of the
carriage is nothing like that of the common hackney carriage.
These are vehicles shrouded in mystery. If you are a connoisseur,
then one look would be enough to recognise these carriages.
Climb in and take your seat. The driver without expending a
word will take you to a white-skinned beauty of a particular class.
In exchange for the silvery glitter of money they will forget your
swarthy looks and sell their bodies effortlessly. But you have to
be dressed like Europeans. Early evening, you will find many
Bengalis hovering about in this area with this intention.

In the evening, foreign ladies of pleasure also appear on the
street. But without a trained eye one cannot set them apart from
the ordinary memsahibs. However a better look clearly reveals
the characteristics of ordinary prostitutes in their cheap and
gaudy attire, the tired eyes, the over-painted powdered faces,
and in their bearing and gait. They can be seen if one sits for
a while in Curzon Park at the corner of Garher Maath. Eden

Gardens is also a major hunting ground for them. There, it is often possible, without much of a trouble, to discover *firangi* beauties in a state of déshabillé with other men, under bushes or trees and under the cover of darkness. I have already mentioned the behaviour of a kind of 'gentlewomen' on the bank of the Ganga in the early hours before dawn. There is no dearth of the same kind of women amongst *firangi*s, Jews, and other peoples in the white town or *saheb-para*. But they only come out in the evening to deprave men. Many of them work at the telegraph office, many are typists, and many more work as 'shop-girls' in the stores run by Europeans. Many of them have husbands too! Those that are independent, having picked up their prey from the streets, return home quietly. And those who are not, for them the men have to arrange an empty house or make some other arrangement. If they get money they don't discriminate between fair and dark complexions, they will enjoy equally with all—accompany them to the theatre or bioscope, have meals with them at restaurants, and go on joy rides in motor cars. Perhaps, satiated and bored after enjoying the close company of whites, they are tempted by darker complexions for novelty. Usually they give themselves over to the embraces of men right inside the cars. At night, in the shadows and darkness of Garher Maath and in the nooks and crannies of the racing grounds, one can easily watch the dalliances of this type of women. White police guards keep a strict watch over them. At times they are caught in unmentionable situations with strangers inside vehicles. Then their harassment knows no bounds. I had once been witness to the misery of one of these women. She was caught inside a car near the strand. Her partner was a white man. And he, getting off the car, shot off for dear life faster than a cannon ball—the woman got apprehended. The merciless beatings of the sergeant left her fair face battered and bloodied.

Prostitutes from different races of the world live in Kareya and Watgunge. But the signs of life are not much visible on the streets of that area. There the theatre of life is played out hidden behind walls. Bengalis very rarely visit. Here, the main actors of the nightly performances are usually commoners—white sailors, soldiers from the Fort, Chinese and Japanese migrants, and Muslims from lower income groups, among others.

Another specialty of the streets of today's Calcutta is the fear of hoodlums and thugs, the hired goons—or the goondas. This kind of 'gentlemen' are very hardworking. They remain engaged in their 'business' even during the day and it goes without saying, at night too. Earlier, northern cities like Kashi and Mirzapur were famous for their goondas, but Calcutta has now definitely surpassed them. Yet the police force here, both in numbers and power is second to none in India.

The honoured kingpins of the goonda community have their haunts in and around Mechhobazaar. Many of them are from the Muslim community and on the count of wealth and property each of them is a Dhan-Kubera—Mammon, the God of Wealth. 'Hindustani' goondas usually reside in the Barobazaar area. Their gangleaders often open a cocaine or gambling den. Another kind of chief or sardar of goondas form gangs whose work is to strip pedestrians of all their belongings or commit dacoities—planned robberies. Over and above this, every Calcutta neighbourhood has some local goondas who are feared like Yama—the God of Death—by the residents.

At night the coffee shops of Mechhobazaar teem with people. Seventy five per cent of those you find in this crowd are of a violent disposition. All murderers, gamblers, goondas, thieves, dacoits and pickpockets gather here to eat, mingle and have a good time; the *coffeekhanas* serve as their social clubs. The fear of the police keep most branded goondas and those who have fled from custody, from showing their faces during the day. So the dark night is their time for enjoyment. After their meals and casual catching up with each other they spread out in search of their prey.

Usually goondas don't oppress their own neighbourhoods. The reason for such benevolence is not any love for the neighbourhood; rather the risks of getting caught are higher. So goondas oppress neighbourhoods different from their own. There is certainly no doubt that at night Mechhobazaar is a dangerous place. However, it is now close to fifteen years that I have been in the practice of walking down Mechhobazaar alone at night, never encountering any danger. Yet, most of the people who are to be seen in this area late at night are violent like the tiger. They are ever prepared to fling an unsuspecting pedestrian to the ground like a used clay cup, smashing their bones with complete ease and little effort. However, I have not been fortunate enough to be in their good books. The murders and fights in Mechhobazaar, which we often hear about, are mostly the result of gang wars among goondas.

There are endless brawls and murders among their lot. I am giving one example. This was about fifteen to sixteen years ago. For years it has been my habit to visit mysterious places—this can be called an ailment. I had a childhood friend whose name I don't want to disclose. But this much I can say, he was born in a respectable Brahman family—his father was a lover of literature and a high ranking government official. Despite hailing from such a lineage, my friend fell into bad company and became wayward. He used to be a habitué in all kinds of goonda gangs. He had a lot of physical strength—I have seen him single-handedly beat back fifteen to twenty Hindustani goondas. One day I requested this friend, 'Take me to a goondas' den'. He agreed, and took me one evening to a house in Gnyaratola. It was a tall double-storied building and there was a booze shop on the ground floor. The house does not exist anymore—it has disappeared under the sway of the city improvement scheme.

There was a narrow lane beside the house. We entered the house through that lane—both the lane and the house were equally dark. The creatures of this place perhaps considered light to be a useless nuisance.

We began to climb up a broken staircase navigating the darkness when a deep voice thundered, asking who we were. But looking all around I could not locate the interrogator, it felt as if the darkness had spoken. I froze with fear and stood still expecting to feel the icy touch of a sharp dagger any moment.

My friend responded quite unperturbed, 'Is it Amir? Hey buddy, don't you recognise me?'

The darkness did not speak again.

Relieved, I climbed right up to the roof of the booze shop with my friend. No lights there too! But because of the natural light of the sky and light from the street, there was a shadowy darkness here.

I saw fifteen to sixteen Muslim men sitting on the roof. Before them were two or three bottles of booze, a few clay cups and a few sal leaves perhaps holding the finger food to go with the alcohol. They were chatting and drinking intermittently. Each of them had something special in his appearance, the sight of which sent a cold shiver down the spine.

My friend flopped down amongst them, and wrapping his arm around the neck of one in a friendly gesture, snatched away the clay cup from another, finishing the drink in one gulp. The rest burst out laughing.

Then the conversation continued, liquor flowed. No one even spared a glance at me. That I had gone there with one of their buddies seemed to be good enough an introduction.

After a while I noticed some trouble break out in one corner of the roof. Hadn't noticed till then—four or five people were sitting there playing, gambling I suppose. As soon as the trouble broke out, one of the men landed a punch on another. The other returned the blow. Within a moment the first man yanked out a knife from the folds of his clothing and lunged at the second man. The second man managed to parry that attack, but the knife sunk deep into his hand.

What happened after that is not clear to me but I saw everyone on the roof, wherever they had been, stand up on their feet. A stream of ugly expletives was unleashed, then they split up into two groups, and a huge fight broke out. In the beginning, I completely froze with fear. Right in front of my eyes I saw one man hit another fiercely on the head with a booze bottle. 'Oh Lord! That did me in!' cried the injured man, spinning round and crumpling to the floor of the roof.

I realised that one should not remain there for a single moment. I ran for the stairs and then heard cries from downstairs—'Police! Police!' My blood seemed to curdle. If I was picked up by the police from here, how would I show my face in polite society? Who would believe that I was here as a spectator?

Suddenly someone pulled me by the hand from behind. I spun around, shocked. It was my friend.

'This way,' he said. And dragging me along, ran to the edge of the roof.

'The police are coming—quick, jump!' And before I could respond, he jumped into the void and disappeared from the roof.

I didn't have the time to think or ponder any more—death or life, whatever fate may hold in store—I told myself and jumped! And next moment landed bang on Mechhobazaar Street. Springing to my feet, I ran for dear life.

Never again did I ask my friend to take me to a goondas' den. I was done with that fancy.

SCENE THREE

CHINATOWN

Chinatown is a 'must-see' Calcutta neighbourhood. The imprint of the racial and cultural peculiarities of Marwaris in Barobazaar, Muslims in Mechhobazaar, and Europeans in Chowringhee are clear enough. In these neighbourhoods, Calcutta has still not completely lost her identity. But go to Chinatown once, you will no longer feel, you are in Calcutta. At night the light and shade, the people, the conversations, the homes and houses will all evoke strangely variegated recollections and imaginations about faraway China in your mind.

Narrow streets meander snake-like through rows of houses. Walking by you will notice on either side, often inside living rooms of single-storied houses looking out to the street with their front doors ajar, a Chinese mother unmindful of passers-by with her bosom unabashedly bare, nursing her baby. Colourful advertisements in the unintelligible pictorial Chinese script hang over doorways, a Chinese roadside singer—a true Tansen at heart—sings strange, unfamiliar melodies from distant lands while somewhere else three or four Chinamen remain engaged in a discussion laden heavy with the characteristic nasal twang. Almost at every step you will notice Chinese inns, contemporary style hotels and restaurants or gambling and opium dens or else a Chinese temple. The atmosphere is quite novel.

Two friends who were experts about Chinatown invited me one day for a meal at a Chinese restaurant. We first went to an authentic Chinese inn. There were two rooms—one for cooking and the other for the guests—but the kitchen was the bigger of the two. An array of prepared food was arranged on the floor, and a few skinned chickens were strung up above. At three corners of the dining room were three small wooden tables. On either side of each table were two very narrow benches, thin like oars—I was told this kind of narrow seating is typical of Chinese inns. A high table at one corner beside the door was laden with food, bottles and jars and utensils; the owner stood in front of the table with a smiling face.

We went and took our seats at a table. An unknown smell, neither repulsive nor enjoyable, began to waft in. At the next table two Chinamen were eating something. From time to time they were raising their bowls to their mouth, using two thin sticks to pick and scoop out some kind of food from it. They spoke to each other from time to time, often turning to throw surprised stares at our faces. It was obvious from their looks that such natty specimens of contemporary Bengal like us didn't quite make regular appearances in these authentic Chinese inns. The facial expressions of Chinamen when they eat, though worth watching, are beyond description.

At my friend's request a Chinese waiter brought us some meat curry served in a small plate, bowls of liquid rice starch, a plate of eatables, either made from potato juliennes or wheat flour, which looked like *jhuribhaja*, and two small sticks for each of us. These sticks are like the fork and the knife for the Chinamen. The dishes served were not too bad.

We came to know that booze was available at a very cheap rate. A single peg of some drink which cost five *sikka*s in other places could be had for five and half *anna*s here. The reason for these low prices was that booze was procured without the knowledge of the excise department. Chinese spirit was also available but this came with a higher price. I guess this good news hadn't reached the ears of Bengali tipplers yet, otherwise this area would be teeming with people by now. It's hard to say what gave them the courage to sell booze so openly. Most probably the owner drove out unknown tipplers who requested a drink.

Next we went to another shop. Don't know who the owner was but his wife welcomed us with a wide smile and prepared cocoa for us herself. This room also had two tables, one on each side. Chinese sweets were displayed on one of these. The other table was very high; on it three or four chubby babies rolled about, sometimes scratching or biting each other. The owner's son-in-law and his young wife stood in front of the table and watched us quietly. This young woman was a mother at a very young age, like most young Bengali women of the times. When we left, the owner's wife walked us to the door and saluted us in farewell. I was fascinated by the courteousness of this foreign lady.

After that we went to another Chinese inn. This was a large well-decorated place. Electric lights glowed inside, a mixed clamour was audible, people rushed in and out, and the Chinese squatted on the chairs, eating their meals. A man was serving while singing at the top of his voice. We went and sat in a corner room which was neat and clean. Many kinds of Chinese dishes were laid out on the table and one could have whatever one wished.

After sampling a few dishes we ordered Chinese tea. A young Chinese woman arrived and placed some tea leaves in Chinese cups which had no handles, poured hot water and covered each with another upturned cup before leaving. After a while, the tea leaves had infused and the tea was ready. But the upturned cups had become so hot, it was impossible to remove these as they too had no handles. I didn't find this method of preparing tea, followed by the tea-drinking Chinese, at all convenient.

A friend acting brave tried to remove the hot overturned cup but how could he? Some tea splashed on the table and then the young Chinese woman noticing our sorry state came to rescue us from our plight. There is neither milk nor sugar in Chinese tea, but I enjoyed it though it smelt like *chirata* leaves (*Swertia perennis*), a herb with bitter tasting leaves popular for its medicinal value. After a while I noticed that many people were coming to take a peep at us. The Chinese beauty must have gone outside and announced that this strange herd of animals had arrived in this room who didn't even know how tea was to be poured and drunk. Whatever be it, we are not to be embarrassed so easily—with serious faces we went on sipping from our teacups as if nothing had happened.

I noticed, that as long as I was there, a solemn-faced Chinaman from the next room kept staring at my face. Though our eyes met several times, he never averted his gaze. Planting his elbows on the table, he continued watching me with those unblinking eyes. I smiled at him a few times, but still not a single muscle of his face, frozen and mask-like, moved. From the way he was looking at me, it seemed as if I was known to him from a past life. What did he want? Was he trying to hypnotise me? I began to feel uncomfortable and breathed a sigh of relief after leaving that room and coming out on the street.

As we went by, I heard the tinkle of money and a murmur of many voices coming from a longish brightly-lit building. Peeping in I found a room full of people and all were Chinamen. Then I came to know that they were gambling. This is supposed to be sanctioned by their religion. If the Chinese don't gamble then it is considered a breach of faith. So the government doesn't stop them even if they gamble in public. Most Chinamen gamble regularly. Recently because of a government order, public gambling, which was a specialty of Chinatown, has come to an end.

Walking down narrow dirty lanes crawling with Mogs, *firangi*s, Chinamen, and Muslim riff-raff, we found two more eateries—these were set up and furnished in the European style. One was named Canton and the other, ChungWah (now a new restaurant called Nanking has also come up). We entered the second one. As soon as we stepped in, a thin and elderly Chinaman with a pale and expressionless face greeted us. Next came a slim young man, with a happy and smiling face.

We sat in a cabin partitioned with burnished wood. Two male waiters arrived—they were Muslims, not Chinese. Looking around I found that this Chinatown eatery didn't have the tiniest bit of an authentic Chinese ambience.

The curtains of a cabin on the other side were pulled back. Inside, a young European lady—a memsahib—with a drink in her hand was rolling amorously with laughter, now twisting and doubling over with her body, dancing gleefully while still on her chair, now indulging in light banter in an inebriated tone with a European man who was hidden from our view. Suddenly, turning her head and noticing my dark skin she excitedly called out—'Manager!' What was the matter, I wondered. As soon as the manager arrived, she asked him to draw the curtains of the cabin; I guess the dark colour of my face was sullying the colours of her merriment. But I knew this class of white *mems* quite well. As she was being treated to drinks and food at this restaurant by a white man, she was pretending to be annoyed by a dark-skinned person, but if tomorrow she heard the tinkle of money in my pocket then this same beauty would be sitting beside me, twisting with laughter in the same manner.

At night, in these two restaurants, the glory of wine and women finds naked expression. This isn't home turf so there is no fear of running into someone they know, which is why many Bengalis and the English come here to spend part of the night in reckless merrymaking. The people here have seen many young men and women rolling under the table with intoxication. Brawls, which are an inevitable consequence of indulging in wine and women, are not new to this area. There is no dearth of European style hotels and restaurants outside Chinatown so very few of the English and the Bengalis come here just for a meal.

Next to Chung Wah is a gambling and opium den, where opium is prepared and served. (It's not there anymore.) But we are forbidden from entering a Chinese gambling den because it's meant only for the Chinese. As gambling is not sacred or part of the religious practice for people from other belief-systems, their presence in this place attracts the police. But my friends are quite influential here. So I got the rare opportunity to have a look inside a Chinese gambling den. On stepping inside the room I saw about thirty to forty men standing or sitting on chairs around a large floor. I know nothing about gambling so I would not be able to say what kind of game they were playing. But what I did notice were the stacks and piles of notes and coins arranged on the floor. From time to time one would push these stacks towards another as they lost or won. I've heard that more than winning, the excitement entailed in uncertainty is what possesses gamblers like a ghost, and that's why they keep on playing even after betting on everything they have. I've seen people betting on horses going mad with excitement; I was expecting to find something similar here too. But even under the harsh glare of electric lights I couldn't discern an inkling of excitement on the faces of these Chinamen. Most of them, with placid faces, their eyes transfixed, were observing the restless dalliance of the Goddess of Fate. Only a few were smiling gently from time to time and that was it. And they were speaking softly too, no sign of excitement in their voices. No doubt gambling is religion for the Chinese, I told myself. We were watching their game with rapt attention when suddenly one of them turned around and said, 'Babu, this place is not for you all.' Without wasting a word, we left.

Right next was the *chandukhana* or opium den. I guess everyone knows that Chinese opium and our own *guli* or opium balls are similar kinds of intoxicants. But the Chinese smoke opium in a pipe resembling a cycle pump while *guli* users have it from a small hookah attached with a tube. Inside the opium den, a Chinaman was lying on a sofa. His body from waist to feet was spilling over on the ground. One look and you would think it was a corpse—there was no sign of life there. In the midst of the trials and tribulations of life, he had won a rare desirable state of obliviousness through intoxication. It is said that opium has to be smoked while lying down otherwise the opium fumes reach the brain so quickly that it impedes enjoyment. After consuming opium for a while the opium smoker cannot move or stand up, at that point he is helpless like a newborn. It is impossible for him even to kill a fly. What a variety of intoxications people indulged in!

After this we came out on the street and bid adieu to this amazing Chinatown of shadowy mysteries, a turf for goondas with its narrow streets, gambling spots and opium dens, the temples, hotels and bars, and the gaggles of Chinese boys, girls, and the elderly. There are similar Chinatowns in every country because the Chinese are a race of vagabonds, not homebound like Bengalis. I've heard that Chinatowns the world over look the same. The Chinatowns of America and England are well known for sinfulness and trouble. The Calcutta Chinatown while not being so dangerous, is not really safe for common people to venture at night. The nooks and crannies of darkness could suddenly light up with the flash of knives or daggers.

SCENE FOUR
PROSTITUTES QUARTERS

The chief protagonists of the night theatre of Calcutta are the prostitutes. There is hardly any class of people in Calcutta which doesn't frequent a brothel. It's difficult to put a figure to the number of prostitutes in Calcutta. This is because there are countless such women who take cover behind various kinds of professions—they don't figure in the census data. For example consider the maids working in the houses of the babus. Many champions of morality do not visit Bengali theatres on the pretext that our playhouses are sullied by the contact with prostitutes. But those maids with whom they are in contact night and day—who are they? Most of them are prostitutes. Many babus enjoy their company within the confines of their homes, and the number of such babus present in every Calcutta neighbourhood is not small.

The main red-light areas of Calcutta are the following— Sonagachhi, Rupagachhi, Joy Mitrar gully, Upper Chitpur Road, Bowbazaar, Kareya, Harkata gully, Hari-Padminir gully, Sethbagan, Notun Bazaar, Mahendra Goswamir Lane, Simla, Phoolbagan, Keranibagan, Sashibhusan Surer gully, Benetola, Garanhata, Dhakapati, Jorabagan, and Malapara gully etcetera. Besides these, there are a few to several prostitutes living in most Calcutta localities. Therefore it can be said that our city is almost possessed by these fallen women. Surely most people of Calcutta pay visits to their houses often, why else are their numbers swelling by the day? So it seems that the Bengali's opinion about 'good character' is not of a high measure. But the Bengali's morality in this matter has never really assumed much of a rigidity at any point in the past. Similar to ancient Greece, till a hundred and fifty years ago, the prostitute's house was the common meeting point of people in the villages of Bengal. The elderly of the neighbourhood would come with their cloth bags containing prayer beads, and the young men would accompany them. There was not a bit of shame or hide-and-seek in this because, in those times, this practice was not associated with any guilt. Having spent part of the evening in various kinds of discussion they would return to their respective homes. So, in those times, the abode of the fallen woman was the most important meeting place—the men's hub of the village. But let's leave the past for now.

There is a class division among the local prostitutes of Calcutta. Those who stand on the streets or the gullies belong to the lowest strata. They usually live in dingy ground floor rooms with clay tiled roofs, amidst grime and darkness. Servants, load-bearers and *chhotolok*—literally 'small' people from the lowest social and economic rungs—are the worshippers of their beauty. The prostitutes of the next higher level live in two-storied mudhouses known as *matkotha*s. They reside in Malapara gully, Dhakapati, Jorabagan among other places. Usually low-rung employees of businessmen, shopkeepers and the rich visit them in search of pleasure. Next are the prostitutes who live in the ground floor of brick houses or *kothabari*s. They are somewhat courteous. Above this category are the prostitutes of Chitpur Road, Harkata gully and Haripadmini gully—they live on the first or second floor of a brick house. Usually clerks and the like keep their sex trade running. The category right above this is the most important. Now this category has two groups—the *bandha*s with fixed clients and the *chhuto*s with several casual clients. The *bandha*s are the most important of the lot. Many of them get a monthly salary of one hundred fifty to three hundred rupees. And a few of them enjoy a stipend of five hundred, seven hundred or even a thousand. The daily takings of *chhuto*s range from eight or ten upto twenty or twenty-five rupees. Those who are experts in song and dance have an even higher daily income, at times going up to a hundred or a hundred and fifty. There is another group of prostitutes in this category who are partly *bandha* and partly *chhuto*. In their case, the regular babus pay a visit on certain days of the week while for the remaining days they are free; for some others, their babus visit for a certain period of time every day, for the rest of the time they can receive whoever they like. The babus who visit at a specific time and date are famously known as the 'fixed-time babu'. The major haunts of high class prostitutes fall between Sonagachhi, Rupagachhi and Simla. The prostitutes of this class are usually expert in singing and dancing. Some are quite educated and they read and admire Rabindranath's poetry. Since they do not torture their bodies beyond a limit, there is no dearth of great beauties among them. Their manners and words are often quite courteous and free of vulgarity. This class of prostitutes does not suffer much of a financial difficulty when they grow old. This is because many ill-fated men, having seated them upon mountains of money, themselves turn paupers and end up in the dust of the street. Then again, when these prostitutes reach an advanced age, their biological or adopted daughters also earn money. The mother's days pass peacefully with the daughter's income. Elderly prostitutes often become landladies of brothels.

Almost every prostitute of all classes have a man of their own, kept like a pet. Among these despicable creatures—these beloveds of the fallen women—there is no dearth of socially respectable gentlefolk. The fallen women feed and clothe them with their earnings. These man-dogs, often because of excessive pampering, become audacious, and mercilessly beat up the very persons on whose earnings they live. But these miserable women still cannot abandon the men—the love of a sex worker runs so deep and true. Despite enjoying such comforts, their sweethearts often disappear and then many prostitutes even commit suicide out of grief. Such suicides are common among their lot. We can understand from this that the heart of a prostitute is not the dry desert we consider it to be, it's really not in such a terrible state. After all they too are human! Why should they be devoid of the feelings of kindness, affection or love? Rabindranath has explained this beautifully in his poem, 'Patita'—

> *Hriday boliya kichu ki nei,*
> *Chherechhi dharam, ta bole dharam*
> *Chherechhe ki more ekebarei?*
> *Nahi ko karam, lajja-saram,*
> *Janine janame satiro pratha,*
> *Ta bole narir narityotuku*
> *Bhule jawa, se ki sahaj kotha?*
> *Ami shudhu nahi shebar ramani,*

Mitate tomar lalasha-kshuda!
Tumi jodi ditey pujar arghya
Ami snopitam, swarga-sudha!
Debotare mor keho to chaheni,
Niye gyalo sobe matir dhela,
Dur durgam manobanabashe
Pathailo tare koriya hela!'

'Don't have I, at all a heart,
Left the righteous path, but has it
completely, kept me apart?
Neither deeds nor shame remain
Ne'er known what it is to be chaste,
But a woman's feminine soul
Could that be so easily erased?
Am not the woman only to serve
Only to whet your lust and hunger,
Had you given offerings of worship
I would've proffered, the heaven's nectar!
None longed for my spirit divine
Took the earthly lump instead,
Away to remote exiles of the mind
Sent her off in pure neglect!'

'Hate the sin, not the sinner'—everyone should remember these words of Christ. These 'sinful' women, they do not just light the evening lamp at the 'gateway to an earthly hell'. If one is keen to know they will find that other than the sin of offering their bodies, as human beings, they stand no less taller than anyone.

No doubt that their only sin is doing a lot of disservice to society. So our sympathy towards them cannot but be blind. Their beauty, and enchantment is breeding sins—thievery, swindling, murder and mayhem—in society every day. This is not so difficult to comprehend if one pays daily visits to the police-court. And then, the mind naturally fills up with unkind thoughts directed towards them.

As soon as evening falls, the beacons of beauty or uncomeliness line up the overhead verandahs of Chitpur Road. They sit decked up, and the homeward bound clerks on the streets take the 'heads-up vow', looking up at them while they walk down. In their effort to observe this vow, they often almost end up under the wheels of passing cars but somehow managing to escape, the vow-takers, like devoted followers, again rest their hungry eyes on the verandah. Blessed be the perseverance which does not fear death. Who says Bengalis are cowards? Right then, many of these red-blooded libertines having chosen a dish for the night, quickly return home, and having washed and cleaned themselves, changed into a fresh evening attire, and cooled down with a little rest, rush out to swoop down on their chosen 'dish' for the night. That the slavish clerks are the chief clientele of the verandah flesh market of Chitpur Road, is indisputably proved by the fact that on the first Saturday of the month, almost no merchandise remains unsold for want of a buyer. However ugly a woman might be, at least for that night, one or another worshipper would have been found.

At night, it's hard to tell from the street, whether the women of pleasure lining the verandahs of Chitpur are pretty or not. Men enter the house, leaving that matter in the hands of fate. The beauties also leaving the outer verandah, come to the corridor inside the house and stand at the doorway of their respective rooms. Some bargaining follows. But how is it possible to bargain without inspecting the goods? Inside most of these houses it is dark as a new moon night even when there is a bright full moon in the sky. At this time, the babus devise an ingenious way which, while preserving their dignity also allows them to inspect the merchandise. They quickly stick a cigarette into their mouth and on the pretext of lighting it, strike a match, and in that flickering light scrutinise the woman as best as possible.

The standard rules of bargaining are like this—

Babu—'Hello, will you entertain a client?'

Bibi—'How long will it be?'

Some say one or two hours. Others demand the whole night. When four rupees is asked for an hour, the babus offer two. When eight is asked for the whole night, the babus offer four. Then an agreement is reached halfway through. If the price being suggested is too low, then, offering an unsolicited advice like, 'No Sir, not possible here. Go to the earthen tiled hutments, the *kholarghor*,' the bibis, waving the ends of their saris and swinging their hips, walk away to stand on the verandah again.

In Sonagachhi and Rupagachhi, those fallen women who are *chhuto*s and are not bound to a single client, do not strain their legs standing on the verandah unless they are starving. Thanks to the kindness of friends, their rooms rarely lie empty. Strangers who visit from outside are also brought in via negotiations with pimps. Whatever price is decided, the pimps get a quarter out of it. If there is a pimp in between, then the babus have to shell out more money. This is because coming through a pimp, one pays ten for someone whose price is eight. If the bibi's services can be sold at a high price then the pimp's takings also go up, so the pimps leave no stone unturned to hike up the prices. Other than the price of the bibi's flesh, the babu has two more fixed costs. A *paan* which costs four to eight annas and a tip of eight annas or a rupee for the bibi's personal help—the bearer. Over and above this, consider the more cunning among these women who switch to a nagging and insistent tone to wangle out money for the dinner that night—for themselves as well as their mothers. In summer if a flower-seller happens to pass by, then an order for eight annas' or a rupee's worth of garlands of the fragrant white *beliphool* or Arabian jasmine is also very common. Beyond these there exists that capricious demand for a free joyride in a taxi to Garher Maath, which costs nothing less than three or four rupees. Most of the babus even if they are miserly at home, turn into modern versions of the generous Karna when they are here, and it is those birds of the night who have recently learnt to fly who turn out to be the biggest spenders. The bibis can't make much headway with the veterans—those familiar to these streets, their bones well-worn out and creaky from experience. But bibis don't take much time to recognise the old hands of sin-street from their manners and attitude, even if they be strangers. Still in such cases there is a quite a bit of sparring among equals, where the bibi tries to burn a hole in the babu's pocket, and the babu warily tries to cut his losses. The bibis mostly win. They are adepts in the many ways of emptying the babu's pocket—turning it into a Garher Maath, the empty fields of the esplanade. For example, a bottle of liquor is brought for the babu. But what will the babu drink from?

Getting the bibi's signal, her bearer pretends to look for a glass around the room for a while and pronounces—'All glasses are broken.' Being left with no recourse, the babu is now compelled to dig into his pocket for money to buy a glass or two. So, if not anything else, the number of glasses in the bibi's room definitely increases. There are many such simple and elaborate means to get the better of the veterans—the old hands of sin-street.

Many believe that money can easily buy the opportunity to spend time with a fallen woman, to step in and settle down with her in her room. They think, these women don't have any preferences. While this belief is not completely unfounded it is not completely true either. Most prostitutes don't allow just anyone to sit in their rooms and even if more money is offered, they don't usually agree to spend the whole night with strangers. But this is most probably out of fear. Can their lives be compared to anything more defenceless? It is beyond doubt that the first and second categories of fallen women refuse to offer themselves even at double the price if they don't like the general appearance of a client. They allow men to 'sit' or turn them away based on their judgment about them being decent or lowlifes. People from the lowest social and economic rung, even if their pockets be full of money, aren't allowed to cross the threshold of their rooms.

I've already mentioned that there is no dearth of humanity in the characters of these fallen women. Here is an example. Parents are unaware how many schoolboys begin to visit these forbidden quarters when they are just fifteen or sixteen years old! In these places there is no shortage of young girls suitable for them, but still some precocious boys not happy even with that, express a desire for young women who are seven, eight, nine or even ten years older to them. But most often their efforts don't bear fruit. Their perverse desires are not satisfied even if they offer extra money. Instead a barrage of scolding forces them to slip out from the place quickly.

Evening is the time for dressing up and bargaining in this market for beauty. The distinctiveness of these quarters of fallen women is not discernible during this time. The babus also have just arrived and perched themselves against the pillows; conversations are yet to turn interesting, and the drink hasn't yet gone to the head. Therefore it's reasonably quiet all around.

But the climate here changes completely after nine o' clock. Following the first and while the second peg is being poured into the glass, the babus begin to see the world through rose-tinted glasses. With the third peg, their bodies seem to get charged with the fresh blood of youth. The music of the harmonium, singing, and hideous cries of applause from every room on both sides of the streets enlivens the neighbourhood. Somewhere the bibi wearing tinkling anklets, setting the glass of drink on her head, gesturing delicately with her eyes, brows, lips and hands, and swinging her body, begins a slow sensuous dance. The babu begins to play the harmonium and the hired tabla player or the babu's flunkey joins him on the tabla, bobbing his head to the beat, and seeing this, flocks of the curious assemble outside the window or the doorway. Meanwhile, on a sudden impulse of intoxication, the babu fancies dancing too. Pushing away the harmonium, he jumps up to join the bibi and standing beside her, he wraps the pleated end of his dhoti around his head like a woman's veil and breaks out in a hoarse voiced song, accompanied by a mad dance. And right after that, getting carried away by emotions, he tries to embrace and kiss the bibi and inevitably the glass of drink on her head falls and shatters to pieces.

'Oh no! My glass is broken.'

'Let it be. You dance!'

'Oh dear! My new glass!'

'Damn your glass! You think I am that sort of a babu? One is gone, you'll have ten more. Hey bearer! Bearer!'

'Huzur', the bearer appears.

'Get a dozen glasses—take this!' A tenner is flung at him, the bearer sniggers and leaves.

'Now come close to me, give me a ...' babu draws his face close to the bibi.

'Oh! What are you doing!'

'No come on, I swear I will die!'

'Oh, bother! Got saddled with a real drunkard! There are people here.'

'Damn it ... people? All of you close your eyes! What, you haven't yet? I shall hit you with this soda bottle!'

The tabla-player, the flunkey and the friends quickly shut their eyes. When from the few faint but tell-tale sounds they realise that the episode of kissing has been safely executed, they slowly open their eyes.

'Sing another song my darling.'

'The way you are screaming, how can one sing in this ruckus?'

'No, no. Here I am sitting quiet, will not utter another word.'

Again the singing starts—

Kete diye premer ghuri, abar keno lotke dhoro!
Ektanete bojha gyache, tomar sutor manja khoro!

'Snapped all ties of this love kite, why again must you grasp!
One long pull was enough to show that your string was much
too sharp!'

'Kulfi-malai and ice,' a lone peddler sings out from the street.
'Ice. Hey you, ice!'

The singing is disrupted again.

Inside other rooms of the house, at this time, fierce quarrels might have broken out between a group of inebriated babus and some other bibi and her mother. In a neighbouring room the 'fixed-time babu' might have appeared at the appointed hour and found some other man in his room, well settled, leaning on a pillow, and at apparent ease. Immediately, the fixed-timebabu begins to slap and beat up the bibi, and sensing more trouble, the other babu bolts like an arrow. The angry shouts of the babu and the howling of the bibi, animate the whole place. Mingling with this are the sounds of female voices singing from other rooms, thunderous rolls of laughter and cries of applause.

Usually scenes similar to these are reenacted every night at the abodes of a fallen woman. This is what they call *amod* or merry-making. This is what babus go mad for. However there are exceptions to this. Truly, in quite a few houses of these fallen women, there is cultivation of serious vocal and instrumental music, and dance. There is hardly any trouble there and the babus are also quiet and decent.

As the night progresses the bibis and babus get more affected by intoxication. By then the tabla player having collected his remuneration, has fled relieved. The tabla and the *baya* roll on the bed, lying on their sides or upended, yet the bibi's singing does not show any signs of stopping. But no one can tell, whether those notes, in a voice distorted by liquor, is really some song or wailing or the cries of some creature hoarser than an owl. The babu also under heavy intoxication dozes off, and from time to time wakes up with a start, opening his eyes wide and crying out expressions of applause—'*Kyabaat!*'—brilliant and out of this world! ...' *Tohfa!*'—priceless ...' *Aa morey jai!*'—Oh that did me in! ...' *Ba bababa—bahut achha!*' ... Bravo! Awesome!

A characteristic scene in these houses at this hour—the rows of pillows now dislodged, lie about in the corners, centre, and around the bed or on the floor, all in a scattered unruly mess. The milk white bedcover, smeared by *paan* spittle, meat curry, half eaten duck eggs, and spilled drinks has turned multicoloured and is rumpled like the wrinkled skin of a very old man. Somewhere on top of it a friend of the babu snores loudly, having passed out from intoxication. On the floor, empty dishes, breadcrumbs, mutton bones, *paan* wrappers, banana leaves and an upturned spittoon are scattered or lie in an entangled mess, and right on top of that the friend of the babu, while still lying on the bed, throws up whatever liquid and solid he had stuffed down his throat, ejecting all in a torrent, quite suddenly, by way of his gullet.

I believe it is proper to draw the curtain over this devilish scene of enjoyment.

The unfortunate prostitute! What unnatural lives they have to lead. Many of the aggressive guests who regularly visit their rooms do not have any kindness or an inkling of sympathy in their hearts—the grotesque outpouring of their merriment is more merciless than a deluge. However the fallen women silently bear with all kinds of smallness and abomination—

their forbearance surpasses that of Shiva's serpent, Basuki. The money for which they do all this is of little worth compared to this unbelievable forbearance. Living this animal life while being human, is beyond my imagination. Over and above this, is the nightly threat to their lives. Often when the doors are opened in the morning, some unfortunate woman is to be found on her bed, poisoned or murdered with some weapon, and all her money and jewellery has vanished with the babus from last night. Who knows what adjective best describes those who kill them mercilessly? I just can't call them murderers—their sins are much graver. It's impossible to conceive such sinfulness.

The daughters of prostitutes cannot but turn into prostitutes too. So they are destined to bear the weight of such an accursed life. But if those who come on their own—having left their families in disrepute—could see a glimpse of the future, they would certainly forsake their dreams of sensual pleasure. For the first few days certain perverted tastes might put up with this kind of life but after that, instead of enjoyment, comes a life of laments and days and nights of burning in a fiery hell. Leave alone humans, even the inanimate cries out under such torture. I can vouch for the fact that the most highly regarded prostitute of the topmost category is also not happy, and she doesn't enjoy offering herself. Have you seen her laughing? Well it is laughter indeed! Even tears are better than this laughter. Here laughter is the veil for sorrow.

That prostitutes are often ugly is because of such unnatural living. In the poisoned air of this place even the blossoming beauty of a Tilottoma withers away in a few days. In my time, I have seen a couple of women from decent households turn into prostitutes. Some of them were striking beauties. Even now I notice a few of them. But I have to turn my gaze away, mortified by their looks. Even the abiding beauty of the prettiest of women who come here, vanishes in days.

Naturally such an atmosphere breeds beastliness. There are certain houses in the prostitutes' quarters of Calcutta which can be called 'hell on earth'. There, certain gangs of men and women run a ruthless enterprise. Their agents roam around the villages of Bengal and the streets of Calcutta. Their business is to lure women away to this place. Often young girls go missing from the streets of Calcutta. They are abducted, brought and hidden in these houses. If the young women do not agree to the evil proposals even after being held there for some days, then they are punished and chastised by different means. Some are locked up and deprived of food, some are beaten up. There are even worse tortures. Many are subjected to sexual violence. Many secrets of this place have become public after the famous Surbala and Gayatri court judgement. So there is no need to add more to this.

These prostitutes' quarters are the playing fields of thieves, dacoits, murderers and goondas. This is because the night birds, who come here to nest for awhile or longer, come loaded. It's forbidden to appear in this place with empty pockets. The rogues who assemble here at night do so to lighten these pockets. It's a rare night when there is not more than one fight, murder, or robbery in one or other prostitute quarter of Calcutta. Hired goondas are also numerous in this area. They get assigned on women-related issues by one side and attack the other.

Crime and murder had become a regular affair in Rupagachhi sometime back. To deal with this, strict police patrolling was initiated, and well-behaved or ill-mannered pedestrians, whoever came under suspicion, were arrested without justification. Even the threat of goondas couldn't screw up the merry-making of the babus, but the fear of getting in the 'good books' of the police was so demotivating that it resulted in something quite astonishing. During this period of police dominance, we went to observe the situation in Rupagachhi at eleven-thirty one night. Just the way the road to Laldighi gets crowded with people and all kinds of vehicles in the afternoon, when offices break for the day, the area of Rupagachhi looks similar at eleven-thirty in the night. But that night we witnessed an astonishing scene. The streets like accursed deserts lay empty and desolate—not a single car, not a single pedestrian, a deathly stillness prevailed! Where was that familiar sound of song, dance and music, where were those upstart 'captain-babu's with ten-anna-six-anna haircuts wearing the sweeping ankle-length punjabis and churidars with wine-tinted vision, where the peddlers hawking their goods in many voices and the solicitous pimps sidling upto pedestrians! As if by chanting a powerful mantra, someone has made them all disappear. Only groups of *lalpagri*s, the red turbaned police, stood like stone statues at intervals along the street. But for them, there were no other signs of life. Not to take chances, we called a policeman and told our reasons for visiting the area, lest they arrest us too and hold us at the police outpost for the night. Don't know whether the police guard believed us, but he didn't take us into custody and kept staring speechless at our faces, eyes wide in astonishment. Perhaps he was wondering what kind of daredevils were these who for no reason, and disregarding the fear of handcuffs, had come to roam this area at night!

We left the main road and entered the narrow lanes which were the major haunts of the prostitutes. The desolateness of this area was more solemn because even the guards were not here. The imposing buildings on both sides stood in stunned silence as if watching each other in a stupefied daze. There was not a single ray of light coming out of any house, every door and window was carefully sealed. Never in my life had I seen Rupagachhi in such a state which was more miserable than a burning ghat—as if this was an abandoned quarter or a deadly pestilence has suddenly finished off everyone and their corpses were still lying scattered inside the rooms of these houses. A stifling, mute terror seemed to be peering from all sides amidst that throbbing grim darkness. My heart began to thump from fear. Above us an owl screeched and it was like the screams of the dead. Oh how unearthly were those screams—they turned my blood cold ... holding our breath, we advanced a few more steps. Voices could be heard from the house next to us—people seemed to be talking in low whispers. These sounds were somewhat reassuring but on hearing our footsteps that thin glimmer of life, like the garbled words of the dying, stopped the very next moment. I couldn't bear it anymore; we hurried out of the gully emerging right under the glare of the police guards. In these ghostly quarters even the police guards looked like friends.

The police hadn't held back from making arrests in Sonagachhi as well. As a result, while the crowd had thinned there too, the condition of that neighbourhood hadn't become as miserable as Rupagachhi. If the police remained as alert in the long run, it would be a great benefit for Calcutta—the sex trade would fold up permanently from this city.

It is not only because of the rogues, but for several other reasons, that innocents also sometimes fall in grave danger in the prostitutes' quarters. And this is quite natural. A close association with one kind of sin will necessarily lead to the contiguity with sins of another kind. Below, I mention an incident as an example. The hero of this episode is now no more, and his name is not unknown in the literary sphere. But obviously, I shall not spell out his real name.

Satinbabu while having a meal with two friends at a restaurant, out of sheer indulgence, imbibed copious amounts of the blessed offerings made to the goddess of wine. It was quite late in the night, close to one o' clock. It wasn't possible to return home in this condition at that hour—what would his family say! So it was decided that they would spend the night outside.

The three friends set out, tottering, their destination—the house of a winsome lady of pleasure.

But at that time of the night, the worshippers of pleasure had already arrived and occupied the rooms of most of these goddesses. Those who still hadn't had that good fortune, didn't pay any heed to Satinbabu's entreaties. After midnight, prostitutes seldom allowed strangers into their rooms, especially if they were in such a drunken state, fear for their dear lives being the reason.

Satinbabu was now in serious trouble. Both home and outside shelters were shutting him out. Still he did not give up. He headed towards the northern part of Chitpur Road while checking the houses on both sides of the street.

Close to Sovabazaar, they suddenly noticed the lone figure of a woman standing motionless, on the roof terrace of a house.

Satinbabu signalled to her from the street saying that they needed a place to stay.

The feminine figure beckoned them to come in.

Breathing a sigh of relief, Satinbabu and his group went in. They felt very pleased having found a shelter after such trouble. That woman's room was on the second floor. The bargaining was quickly got over with. They entered the room and settled down relaxed on a mattress spread on the floor.

Then they focused their efforts on getting a conversation going. But the conversation didn't quite take off. The beauty seemed to be overwhelmed in some thought. Giving brief answers to some questions, she suddenly left the room closing the door behind her, saying, 'Please wait. I will just be back.'

Satinbabu waited for sometime but the lady did not return. He called out loudly a couple of times, but no response. So he rose and tried to go out but the door wouldn't open. It had been chain locked from outside!

Slightly surprised, Satinbabu stood wondering when his glance fell on the bed! Someone was lying on the bed, wrapped in a sheet from head to foot. And what were those spots on the sheet? Satinbabu bent down to look—it was blood!

His heart froze! He asked the friends to have a look. One of them pulled up a corner of the chador and screamed, letting it go immediately.

'What did you see?' Satinbabu asked in a voice laced with fear.

'Corpse! With a slit throat!' the friend managed to croak.

They began to tremble. The intoxication vanished in moments.

With great difficulty, Satinbabu controlled himself and again asked, 'Male or female?'

'Male!'

Now what? There's a corpse inside the room and the door is locked from outside. Surely this was meant to land them in trouble. They shouldn't waste another moment here but there was no way of escape!

Satinbabu rushed to the verandah. He peered out and found that right next was the roof of another house. He called out to his friends, jumped and somehow landed on that roof. The friends didn't waste a moment and followed suit. They went from one roof to another and then down the stairs of a house. This too was a brothel and therefore no one who saw them, suspected anything on seeing these strangers.

On hitting the street, they saw a group of police guards briskly passing by—headed towards that dreadful house. A little more delay and they would have ended up in their hands.

Most probably the murderer had slipped away after committing the act and to save her own skin this woman had planned to implicate these three innocents. It could be none but she who had informed the police.

SCENE FIVE

NIMTALA BURNING GHAT, THE CREMATORIUM

Life is farcical even though it ends in loss. Having sent off a young son to the crematorium a woman gets pregnant before the turn of the year; in a country where the girl child is considered a burden, a poor clerk—father of seven daughters—cannot desist from continuing to have a sexual relation with his wife; putting living creatures on the sacrificial altar, men worship the inanimate as conscious; having spent the whole life in penury, the miser goes on accumulating wealth which others would squander away— how many more should I mention? In every passage of the book of life there are such innumerable scenes of farce. So when at the end of their acts, the bodies of these actors burn defencelessly in the funeral pyre at Nimtala, it seems that a play is being staged, which by no means, is one with a tragic ending.

From time to time, I have visited the Nimtala burning ghat late at night. On many an occasion, I have witnessed a strange variety of scenes which are difficult to put into words. I had also gone to Kashi Mitra ghat once but have vowed never in my life to venture there again. A vehicle from the Medical College had brought a number of corpses dissected by doctors—cut up, swollen, disfigured and stinking. These were being burnt. Oh, I haven't seen such a fearsome sight anywhere again. I had run away from that place. I couldn't sleep the whole night. Thinking of it gives me the shivers even today. I hear that recently a better system has been introduced there for cremating corpses.

Those who live within the premises of the crematorium surely become cold-hearted; their souls get hardened like calloused feet. You will find that the pyre, on which just a while ago a human body had turned to ashes, is being used by someone to cook a pot of rice. The pyre which has devoured the flesh of one becomes the means for providing nutrition to another. People will consume this rice unperturbed. I cannot imagine this—so much insensitivity towards the death of a fellow human! I vividly remember one particular day. I had gone to watch a play at Minerva. The first act had just got over. I had stepped out for a bit for some cool fresh air. Suddenly I saw a funeral procession carrying a corpse going down the street. Part of a black naked body was hanging free from below the bed perhaps because the knots in the rope had somehow broken or come undone. Gaslight and the lights from the theatre were brightly lighting up the corpse. The dangling body swayed with every step of the pall bearers.... I entered the theatre hall. But setting my eyes on the stage, I again saw that black, naked, half-exposed, swaying corpse. I couldn't watch the play any longer that day.... When students of the medical college dissect corpses, the smell of the rotting dead do not leave their hands that day, even after a thousand washes. Yet, they effortlessly have their meals using those hands. I would have died from starvation. I had fainted after watching a dissection at the newly built police hospital on Amherst Street. For the following few days I had fasted, hardly touching any food. Don't know why, but whenever I sat down to eat, I would remember that scene—the stiff corpse lying prone, arms and legs spread wide, and someone with a sharp instrument scooping out something from his back.

On my nocturnal visits to the Nimtala burning ghat I have seen laughter and tears co-exist. The solemnity that we find in the final resting places of people from other religions is missing in the burning ghats of Hindus. It is also missing in our funeral processions. There is a feeling of respect towards the dead in the funeral processions of Christians or Muslims, but it doesn't seem we have anything of that sort. Often I find the bearers of the dead lay down the cot with the body, on the street, to get a drink or buy a bottle from a liquor shop. Many bear the corpses smilingly, chatting along the way. And our shouts of *Bolo Hari Hari Bol* are quite terrible. Sometimes it sounds like a monstrous ridicule. Hindus I guess are all philosophers from birth. When life itself is transient why split hairs over death? But I will leave instructions before my death that no one should utter *Haribol,* when taking my body to Nimtala.

A visit to Nimtala burning ghat shows us how, amidst the scenes of death and the confluence of mourning, quite delightfully indeed, a kind of relaxed adda—comprising idle talk, exchange of socio-political views and gentle sparring—congeals, swelling up more at night than the day. Mothers who have lost their sons, women who have lost their husbands, and children who have lost their parents, wail relentlessly, tearing the sky apart; the corpses of the destitute and the rich, master and servant, wise and stupid, children and the old, lie around, the pyre blazes away and human bodies nurtured with so much affection and care, some of them paragons of beauty, such storehouses of talent, the only resorts of many helpless people, turn into ashes before our eyes. The priest chants mantras, the young widow like a madwoman touches the dead husband's lips with fire, some pour *shanti jol*—the holy water for peace—over the pyre, a teary-eyed son who has just lost his father haggles for pennies off the undertakers' fees, the chants of hymns and prayers rise from the temple of Sasaneswar Siva—the presiding deity of the burning ghat—here and there groups sit and consume liquor or smoke ganja—they are immersed in high-pitched bantering, cracking of jokes and laughter. A sanyasi has settled down at one corner and in front of him a group of followers—having lost their intelligence and the faculty of reasoning—sit and listen to his bluffs with folded hands while on another side a police guard dozes helplessly, dreaming of the smiling face of the women selling *paan*—her forehead adorned with a coloured spot of bindi. On the bank of the Ganga a group of waggish youngsters indulge in pranks and playful mischief. One, sitting on the ghat, has fallen into a meditative trance with his eyes closed, while another has broken into a hoarse-voiced song—

'Shashaan bhalobasish boley shashaan korechhi hridi!'
'You love the burning ghat so I turned my heart into one!'

Having witnessed these amazing scenes, it becomes clear that the prevailing mood of a Hindu crematorium is not one of sadness and mourning. In fact there seems to be an excess of commotion embedded in the mood and character of this place. What does the world care that you've lost your dear child ... that the light of your eyes has been put out? It will go on as it always has—without even turning to look in your direction. It will not stop laughing on hearing you cry. This harsh truth of life is revealed on a visit to Nimtala.

Once a *sanyasini*, a female ascetic, had arrived from somewhere and settled down in Nimtala. I heard her name on Calcutta streets and saw her photograph in *The Statesman*. People who are easily swayed by passing fancies started such a huge campaign for a few days that I went to see her one night. She was sitting quietly on the other side of the crematorium, facing the river. As far as I could see, the distinguishing feature of her appearance was that it was difficult to say whether she was a man or woman. I couldn't comprehend what kind of talent had brought her so much popularity. The people, as if waiting for a morsel of her mercy stared at her rapt, but it didn't seem that they had deciphered the secret of her talent. Right then another *sanyasini* arrived there. She was about twenty-five. She was clad in a blood-red sari, her hips swung heavily at each step, and her hair lay open on her back. In her mannerisms, bearing and aspect there was no hint of any asceticism but only an ugly playfulness. A few more people arrived with her, maybe her devotees— whether they were worshippers of her yogic powers or her youth, was unknown to me. The young *sanyasini* immediately struck up a fierce quarrel with the one mentioned earlier. Oh what vile and obscene language was exchanged, one has to shut his ears to it. Initially I couldn't understand the reason for the quarrel. Finally I came to know that this young *sanyasini* had earlier established her exclusive authority over this crematorium, but with the arrival of the new *sanyasini* her market has been severely affected, this was supposed to be the reason for the dispute. I went to Nimtala burning ghat one night, a few days later. The famous newcomer *sanyasini* had vanished, but the young ascetic was conspicuously present there, in full glory. She was bantering with some men. One cannot say for sure, but there seemed to be the colour of intoxication in her eyes.

Prostitutes often come here at night for pleasure walks. They can only tell, what exactly they come to see. They are mere worshippers of the body. Do they enjoy watching this terrible end for the human body? Amazing! This is a peculiarity only possible among Hindu Indians, prostitutes of other religious persuasions, would never participate in this. They are but creatures of pleasure and enjoyment—disease and death are eyesores for them. The prostitutes arrive tottering with intoxication. They are accompanied by some debauchees—their licentiousness stamped on their features. Their shocking and obscene delirium of lust and licentiousness doesn't stop even on entering this place. Moving around watching cremations, making obeisance to the deity at the temple of Sasaneswar, and offering small contributions, they leave this abode of mourning resounding with their laughter, jokes, and the commotion of defiled enjoyments!

Sometimes the prostitutes bring their own dead. They arrive almost half naked, wearing only a piece of cloth. They are also completely sloshed. The silence of the night is torn apart by the shrill cries of *haribol* in their high-pitched girlish voices, and those whose homes are near the burning ghat, know very well how the mind begins to suffer a kind of unease on hearing those cries. The soul of a luckless woman has been released from the cage of a body worn out by numerous assaults, sorrow, insults, meanness and the weight of nasty diseases—this body, cold in death, does not display any signs of lust or seductiveness. But her companions don't bother their heads over such thoughts, they are not the least subdued by the sights of the crematorium and man's final end—they get drunk and quarrel with each other, they direct humorous obscenities at their deceased companion or else they indulge in coquettish and amorous frolicking with some other man at the crematorium. This is very unnatural indeed.

Small assemblies take place on some nights at the burning ghat. From football and cricket to collectivism and politics, no subject is left out. There, corpses are burning one after the other, and here, chatting and arguments continue unperturbed—isn't this incongruous? In almost every Calcutta neighbourhood there is a group of people who, while not still professionals, are given the duty to bear corpses of the dead of the locality. Their minds are not seized by any grief for the dead, so putting down the corpses many of them join these assemblies mentioned before. A few of them, having borne the dead for a long time, have become seasoned experts in this job. And they have a stock of amazing stories related to cremation of corpses. Some of these stories are startling and quite astonishing. I am narrating one such tale. I had heard this from an elderly corpse bearer at Nimtala burning ghat. I am not responsible for its veracity or otherwise but the storyteller had said that this was a true incident. This is how it goes—

We live in an old locality of Calcutta (he had mentioned its name which I can't recollect). We are summoned whenever someone in our neighbourhood dies, and there is a shortage of corpse bearers. We have become famous in the neighbourhood for cremating the dead. The only bit of self-interest that we have in this activity is that, following social norms, the relatives of the dead invite us for a meal another day.

A few years ago, one night we were sitting and chatting when suddenly an old man entered the room. He told us that a woman had died in his house but because of lack of people who could help, her cremation was not happening. We didn't know this old man. In Calcutta neighbourhoods, everyday new tenants arrive, and it's not possible to know everyone. But without any objection, we tightened our belts, took our cotton bath-towels and followed the old man.

The old man took us to a house in a dark lane, right at the edge of the neighbourhood. The house, like the old man, was worn and dilapidated from the weight of many years. It was pitch dark inside. No signs or sounds of life. It was just like a haunted house, a cold terror stirred up inside you soon as you entered.

The old man opened the door to a room on the ground floor. An earthen lamp was glowing dimly almost at the point of burning out. It was there as if to reveal the depth of the darkness inside the room. In that shadowy darkness we saw a corpse lying on a rope cot, it was covered with a sheet. The whole room seemed to be replete with an unnatural smell of death.

We brought out the cot with the body but the old man kept standing inside.

'Hey Sir, come,' I said.

'If I go who will keep watch over the house?' the old man said.

'Sir, how can that be! It's your dead, how can we take it if you don't come with us?'

'Okay then. Let's start. I am coming along,' the old man said with great reluctance.

We proceeded towards the burning ghat with the corpse, the old man followed. When we had arrived at Beadon Street, suddenly, a drop of something cold fell on my throat. Had it started raining? But looking at the sky I saw not a speck of cloud there. I wondered, taken aback a little when another drop trickled down. Must be something dripping from the cot! ... But what could it be?

I began to feel agitated. I called out to my companions and told them about this. Then what we saw under the light of a gas-post stiffened our legs as if we were struck by paralysis! Blood, blood—it was blood dripping down the sheet covering the dead! But where was this blood coming from?

We quickly turned around but couldn't see the old man anymore. He had slipped away at some opportune moment.

Now what? Had the one we were carrying along been murdered? As we were on the street, we didn't feel confident to remove the sheet and check—what if someone noticed? Astounded, we stood there with the bed of the dead on our shoulders—we could neither proceed nor retreat. If we turned back and went to our neighbourhood with the corpse, people would be suspicious. And if we went ahead to the burning ghat we would be caught.

'Let us abandon this here and run for our lives, whichever way we can,' one of us said.

'Then we will be immediately arrested. There you see, a police guard is watching us,' I said.

Our hearts began thumping loudly but still we went ahead, our lives at stake. It's not necessary to discuss in detail what went through our minds as we passed right under the eyes of the police guard. Thankfully, the guard didn't utter a word. We had been delivered from the immediate danger but what would happen at the burning ghat? It would be impossible to evade all eyes and burn this bloodied corpse there. Nothing could save us anymore.

We arrived at Nimtala burning ghat like men possessed. It was pretty late in the night. At every step we felt we were moving, a step at a time, towards the gallows.

In great desperation we stepped inside. Without looking anywhere, we walked blindly and straight up to the area of the burning ghat close to the bank of the Ganga. Putting down the cot and pulling up a corner of the sheet covering the corpse we found what we had expected. Someone had murdered this woman.

Thank our lucky stars—that night, this part of the burning ghat was deserted. Without waiting a second more, we left the cot with the corpse right there and one by one dived into the Ganga. Then after one long swim we climbed out and up the shore at quite a distance.

Returning to our neighbourhood we rushed back to that house. It was empty. We haven't seen that old man ever again.

SCENE SIX
HOTELS AND RESTAURANTS

'Hotels', which are actually eateries or restaurants referred to as 'hotels' in local parlance, cannot be left out from the night scene of Calcutta because eating out at restaurants is a modern fashion of the *sakher-babu*s.

There are many categories of eateries in Calcutta but it is meaningless to discuss all of these here. Because usually those which are popularly known as 'Hindu hotel or eating house for gentlemen' are absolutely lacking in any specialties worth describing. Usually poor gentlefolk family-men and groups of employees of local *gaddiwala* businesses in the unorganised sector have their meals there and it's an exceedingly prosaic sight. Nowadays many tea shops have also achieved 'hotel' status but their hours extend till evening at the most, and students of schools and colleges or poor clerks, acting as their patrons, keep them in business. Another category of 'hotel', with big ungrammatical English or French names, can be spotted especially near theatre halls. These hotels are confined to one-storied single rooms. Here the food is prepared and displayed right next to the street while dust, dirt, bits of garbage and all kinds of insects land on the displayed food items. Here the waiters, much like the shopkeepers of Radhabazajar, holler at customers, trying to attract them to commit suicide by partaking of this poison-like food. Not even by mistake would the *sakher-babus* set foot in these places. Just as cockroaches (despite having wings) are not birds so too these are not really restaurants, they are commonly known as '*chaier dokan*' or tea shops. However a few of these are miniature versions of the real 'hotels' (restaurants) but being too public, they lack that air of mystery.

While there are not too many big hotels in the Indian neighbourhoods of Calcutta, the number of mid-range hotels are not few. However, in matters of grandeur, quality and cleanliness, most of them don't measure up to the smallest of the hotels and restaurants of the *saheb-para,* the neighbourhood occupied by the Europeans. Yet they are not short of customers. The arrangements in some of these places are quite appalling. In some others one finds that while there hadn't been any lack of care, effort, and expenditure on the part of the owner, there is a severe lack of good taste in the decor. While the interiors are amply decorated, yet everything seems to have been done following an unenlightened tradition or aesthetics, which means there is an excess of elements but no art.

The distinctiveness of these hotels and eateries are not at all noticeable in the daytime because like prostitutes, they wake up and begin their day as evening falls. Then electric lights come on in their rooms, the electric fans spin speedily and everything is decked up and put in order as far as practicable. There is a somewhat close connection between the Bengali's 'hotel' visits and his visits to a brothel. So the number of hotels and restaurants in Sonagachhi is large. Other than the presence of prostitutes, two other distinguishing characteristics of this area are eateries and *paan* shops.

The hotel authority doesn't allow bars in Indian neighbourhoods, but this impediment has been watered down in practice. The principal guests of hotels in the Sonagachhi area are those who enjoy their drink and one cannot say for sure that many hotels do not sell liquor freely but clandestinely. In the public areas of the hotel you might find a notice saying 'Bringing alcohol is prohibited', but if you peep into the private rooms you will notice more and more emptied liquor bottles being sent out. Some hotels and restaurants may not be selling booze; however it's impossible to run a hotel in this area if it doesn't at least allow people to consume spirits within the premises. When most of the customers here are drunks, the hotel owners are forced to turn a blind eye, and they can't be really blamed for it. The authority is against having 'bars' within hotels but the secret practice of selling liquor is quite rampant here. As a consequence, the poor drunks turn out to be the biggest losers—if they buy their booze after eight in the evening, they have to pay a rupee extra on every pint.

Out of all eateries located near theatre halls, the most neat and clean and well decorated ones are Minerva Restaurant on Beadon Street and Minerva Grill in front of Star Theatre. Both are owned by the same person. Here, the quality of food and cooking is better than all 'hotels' located in Bengali neighbourhoods. The customers of these two restaurants are often people from distinguished and aristocratic families. But liquor-lovers would be disappointed for one reason—booze is not sold here on the sly.

The eateries of Sonagachhi get customers mainly during two different times of the day. In the evening when babus step out on their hunt for beauties they often come to a 'hotel' to begin with. They first settle down with liquor and a few dry snacks—meat dishes mostly—to get 'acclimatised'. During this time they discuss which direction they should take to get the best game. Another category of customer arrives much later in the night—they come in pairs, Misters and Misses together. In the restaurants of the white town or *saheb-para* there is no dearth of decent women guests. But decent womenfolk don't step into any hotel or restaurant of the Indian neighbourhoods, the exceptions being Minerva Grill and Minerva restaurant. So while trying to emulate the *firangis*, the babus have to make do with sad excuses of the original. Just like the 'fallen women', the hotel owners too, get the maximum number of customers on the first Saturday of the month. There is another similarity between the hotel owners and the fallen women. Their business also involves pandering to the tastes of others, controlling everyone with sweet words, and tolerating various kinds of torture with a smiling face.

The standard script for the nightly performances which play out in the hotels of Sonagachhi area is somewhat like this. A group of babus arrive for a meal. The owner greets and welcomes them in and sends them to a 'room' or a snug—a partitioned space or a curtained private cabin with tables and chairs. As soon as the babus settle down, the bearer arrives. Immediately an order is placed for some 'dry' dish of snacks, a bottle of whisky or brandy, some ice and a few bottles of soda. The bearer delivers the order soon enough.

While the liquor is poured into each glass, one of the babus pipes up, 'No brother, please excuse me today.'

'Not done!'

'No, no, I have to return home early—I fear they will smell it on my breath.'

'Oh I see! Turned into a 'good boy' is it—don't be so virtuous!'

'No Sir, you won't understand. If the wife finds out, she will immediately hang by a rope, or take opium or douse her body in kerosene and set fire to herself.'

'Good riddance! The lucky man loses his wife! Why are you scared? Now take this; don't be a naysayer and spoil the party by singing off-key!'

The glasses get empty, more liquor and soda are poured. The man who was resisting earlier, does so this time too but not with the same vigour. During the third round he doesn't resist at all, and on the fourth he himself pours his drink from the bottle. The psychology of a drunkard is quite amazing. Just as the tiger, having tasted blood, becomes more ferocious, the drunkard also having given in to temptation doesn't know the limit any more. At that point he is constrained to drink even against his wishes.

With increasing intoxication the babus' voices begin to rise to higher scales. At that point it's difficult to comprehend what they are talking about. Sometimes it is about the *barobabu* or the saheb at office, sometimes about the wife, sometimes about the 'torture' inflicted by their parents, and in between there are high-pitched cries of 'boy', orders for more food or a line or two of table-thumping songs.

'Let's go to Dalim's house,' one suggests.

'No, that bint is too full of vanity—she has her nose up in the air. I am not prepared to tolerate such vanity after having paid out of my pocket!'

Another voices his protest saying, 'No, no, Durga Pujo is close at hand, I am not going to cross her threshold now—she will suddenly come up with some capricious demand.'

'Let her! Where will you get such beautiful eyes and that wondrous smile?'

'Damn the eyes and the smile, money can even fetch tiger's milk, and you are talking about the eyes and the smile?'

Dalim's fan having lost the vote, sighed loudly and proceeded to fill his glass.

'Better to go to Chine-Chameli's house; she will blow our minds away with song and dance!'

'And the rate is cheaper ... '

'Knows the worth of gentlemen ... '

'But Dalim ... '

'You mention Dalim again and I will break this soda bottle on your head!'

'Boy, boy! Bill *le aao!*'—'Get the bill ... '

The babus then set out for the garden where Chine-Chameli has blossomed. In a while another thirsty and hungry group arrives and takes possession of another cabin of the 'hotel'. In this group there are four men and two women. The women are dressed like adherents of Brahmoism. They have a cloth tied over their heads which is a new fashion among the modern age ladies. These two women have picked this up from them. Both sport eyeglasses and have golden *lapeta*—the latest fashion and a cross between the 'pump' shoe and the Mughal style *nagra*—shoes on their feet. Prostitutes camouflage their identity so expertly that at first sight many of them might be mistaken for educated modern women. But in most cases their jewellery, nose rings and the golden shoes give away their true identity.

Everyone in the new group had already had enough to drink before arriving here. Still they are not satisfied, because surprisingly they are still able to move about and walk! '*Mawd, mawd*'—they cry out for liquor and promptly one of them takes out a small bottle of whisky from his pocket and puts it on the table. Immediately three bottles of soda and a slab of ice arrive and the singing starts. The effect of double intoxication becomes apparent within half an hour. One of them with drooping eyelids suddenly embraces a woman saying, 'Angur, I love you so much.'

'Oh dear me, his passion brims over!' Angur says, twisting her shoulders playfully.

'So you don't trust my words dear,' the first man says in a tone of hurt, 'Okay then watch this, whether I can give my life for you at this moment or not!' And so saying he picks up the table knife in his hand.

Immediately the three other men join the chorus, echoing his words to proclaim their love, 'Angur, I love you so much!'

'Enough, enough … do you want your wife to wipe off her streak of marital bliss—the vermilion from the parting of her hair—and have vegetarian food for the rest of her life, because of me? I don't ask you dear to give your life, better buy me a collar of pearls! Then I will know the depth of this love of yours.'

The first lover, pretending not to hear her, pleads with the other woman, 'Hena, please sing a song darling!'

'But how can I sing inside a hotel?' Hena retorts.

'Of course! You *shall* sing!'

Not bothering the drunks any further, Hena begins to hum—

'Didi, lalpakhita amae dhore de na re.'
'Didi, please catch that red bird for me.'

One of the men begins to keep the beat using the table like a tabla, another taking two glass tumblers begins striking them against each other mimicking the notes of cymbals and the babu who was about to sacrifice his life, rises to dance, only to topple over onto the floor where he keeps lying still. While making music, one of the glasses shatters to pieces, the bits raining all over the lover but the one who broke the glass, the one on whom the pieces landed, and the ones who watched, none feel the need to be least bothered about it.

Suddenly a loud wave of singing and laughter is heard from up the stairs. Voices of twelve or thirteen women float up at the same time! The singer, musicians and listeners of this room quickly peep out to find a flock of dusky, fair and brown-skinned 'fairies' climbing up the stairs but there was not a single man in this group of women!

'Matal Hari!' Angur said.

'Matal Hari' was a famous woman captain of Calcutta, similar to the captain-babus who were men. She was not at all good to look at, but she made pots of money from singing and squandered it all away. She had a strange whimsicalness. As soon as she received a payment, she shut down her business for a few days and went around town in a merry-making spree with a group of women known to her. The merry-making continued as long as the money lasted; she didn't usually invite male friends in this merriment. Day and night she drank and alongside that weed, opium and guli was also not left out. While our 'Matal Hari' name was imaginary, there was actually a real person like this.

Matal Hari and her companions sat down ostentatiously in a big room. The entire 'hotel' building rang with the din of feminine voices. The hotel owner looked very happy. With the arrival of a customer like Matal Hari, there was no doubt left in his mind that all the food would be consumed that day. He quickly went upstairs and smiling widely said, 'What would you like to have dear Hari, order it!'

'Brother! Why should I order, while you are here? You can order on our behalf and tell them what we like. Do come and join us … we are not letting you go!'

By and by the tables fill up with liquor and soda bottles, glasses, ice buckets and food plates; tuneless singing, peals of laughter, mad dancing, the smashing of plates and glasses, shouting in vulgar language, and obscene conversations—who dare keep ears open amidst this! Some new customers quietly slip away seeing all this, but some of those who are not scared away are drawn in by Matal Hari to her group. By then, Angur and Hena also join Matal Hari's party, but their male friends escape, having never witnessed such things with their own eyes. Only the 'lover' hasn't given up on the opportunity to offer himself. After a while, he raises himself from his bed of glass shards and arrives on all fours to sit beside Angur, expressing his love for her from time to time.

This scene may be new for this restaurant but people like Angur and her lover are to be found in most restaurants ('hotels') of Calcutta's infamous Sonagachhi area.

It's not possible to run an eatery in this area unless the owner is quite formidable. Where most of the customers are drunkards, there is always the possibility of mishaps and all kinds of trouble breaking out. And so they do. Maintaining peace here is not the job of a mild-natured man.

The food in these restaurants is not prepared to cater to ordinary tastes. Drunkards frequent these places and they love food spiced with chillies. So the dishes here are overly spiced and hot. And then in some hotels the food is so hot and spiced up with chillies that unless one is intoxicated out of his senses, one would not be able to push this food down the throat.

It is not that the food in these 'hotels' is of a good quality. Often it is adulterated. The ghee is of a poor quality and some even use groundnut oil. Leftovers of meat from today are put to good use tomorrow. And because beef is cheaper, certain hotel owners have been arrested for passing it off as goat meat. If drunkards had been in their senses then most of Calcutta's hotels and restaurants would have closed shop by now from a lack of customers.

SCENE SEVEN
FESTIVE NIGHTS OF CALCUTTA

Despite the miseries and the crushing poverty all around, when Calcutta laughs, she laughs heartily. But over the days this laughter has been dying out. The cheerful face of Calcutta that we had seen on festive nights during our childhood is not visible anymore. There is a world of difference between the celebration of religious and social festivals twenty-five to thirty years ago, and the present. And the main reason for this difference is that, in those days a little money could buy a lot of merriment and now more money fetches less of the festive cheer. The suffering poor are always more in number, but nowadays the numbers of the rich have also decreased. More importantly, the new rich are not big-hearted like those of the past. The rich people of those days were not satisfied only with their own pleasures, they would bring ten others along to share in their fun and merrymaking. The rich of our present times mostly desire their own pleasures; they are not much bothered about the ten others.

Durga Puja, the four-day long ritual worship of the mother goddess Durga, is the most important festival of Calcutta just as Muharram is for the Muslims. But the number of Durga idols is gradually decreasing nowadays. Till seven or eight years back Pathureghata (Pathuriaghata) used to trump all other localities in the celebration of Durga Puja festival. Still the number of idols that is seen in this locality is not to be found anywhere else. Earlier, the streets of Pathureghata would be teeming with people on the day of the immersion. This was because many processions for immersion of the idols would come out almost simultaneously, and this was a sight worth watching.

On the nights of Durga Puja, rivers of people seem to flow through Pathureghata—crowds follow crowds, following more crowds, there's no end to these comings and goings. The streets are radiant with garlands of light. The *dhaak*, dhol, and the festive cheer-inducing notes from the *nahabat* resound through all quarters. There is a smile on every face and everyone is dressed in new clothes. During this time, everyone is free to enter the houses where Durga is worshipped, and from evening till night, groups of people come to view and behold the idol of the Goddess. There are enough women in these crowds. Girls from the families of poor gentlefolk also come to see the idol and of course prostitutes do too. Prostitutes love crowds because crowds make it is easier for them to pick out their prey. So to slay men they turn up fully made-up and dressed to kill, and move around among the hordes of people. There is never a dearth of 'talent' and 'skill' in a crowd and among these hordes too there exist 'talented folk' of different kinds. Some come here only to behold what is beautiful. Right from prostitutes to the veiled faces of gentlewomen, following them into the inner chambers of these houses, their eyes remain ever alert—as soon as they notice a remarkable face, their eyes get transfixed. This category of 'skill', though coarse and indecent, is safe. This is because, beyond visual satiation, they lack the courage to make any further advances. The second kind of 'talent' desires both to see and to touch. Like crows waiting expectantly for crumbs of food offerings in a holy place, they wait in front of the gates of the house which has maximum grandeur. Groups of gentlewomen and those not so gentle or cultured come and go. Whenever these men see someone they fancy, they join the group. Beyond the gates of the house, there is usually a narrow passage. When crowds pass through this stretch, there is inevitably some pushing, jostling and brushing against one another going on. The 'talents' endowed with special skills look forward to this because this opportunity to brush past mind-blowing beauties thrills them from inside, stirring up their bodies. They go in with the women and come out with them. Then they again wait outside the gate for a new group to arrive. I have seen one 'famous professor of English' from Calcutta, in such a group. The third category of talent is even more advanced. They use this opportunity to ruin women from socially respectable families. The fourth category of talent comes here to choose prostitutes—they too are not a threat to commoners. The fifth kind of talent is not bothered with the study of beauty. Little girls come to see the deity and these people steal girls if they can get them in their clutches. In the sixth category of talent we can count in the thieves, cheats, pickpockets and goondas. It is because of their good graces that many find necklaces, ear ornaments or the money in their pockets, disappear. There is such a variety of talent in the crowds, but it is a difficult task to recognise their true nature in festive gatherings. There is no count of the numbers of people whose festive joy is transformed by them, every year, into the depressing shadow of grief. On the night of the immersions, the banks of the Ganga and the nearby streets of Calcutta fill up with crowds.

These crowds of people, wearing clean new dresses, are a pleasure to watch. This is surely a day for bonding—for embracing even the enemy as a friend. This is why there is a hint of softness, calmness and delightfulness in every face; scenes of *kolakuli*—the traditional style of embracing—and the exchange of namaskars are to be seen on every street. Later that night it's more common to come across groups of people who have consumed the intoxicant *siddhi*, rather than drunkards. Many of them have constricted pupils, they laugh loudly for no reason, talk deliriously and the signs of fatigue soon become prominent in their bearings and mannerisms. That day a lot of minors go above limit in their consumption of *siddhi* at some friend's place and then fearing scolding from their parents, cannot return home. So they are compelled to roam about the streets late into the night.

On Diwali night, a vista of human heads are to be seen crowding Chitpur Road, especially between the Chorbagan and Mechhobazaar crossings. One would notice that a desperate effort has been made to decorate the roadside shops with garlands of light and inexpensive drawings done by bad artists. Though there is not an iota of any enticing speciality in these decorations, the people on the street stand and gape wide-mouthed at these. I've been noticing from my childhood that every year all the shops are decorated in a similar fashion. As if this excessive sameness of decoration is publicly mocking the strange newness of the present. On Diwali day, the sweets in the confectioners' shops are also decoratively stacked in a special manner.

Above the garlands of light, the beauty of the verandah-belles have not been devoured tonight by the mischievous darkness. Wearing colourful printed saris and sleeveless blouses, powdering (chalk or lime if powder is not available) their necks and arms, applying rouge (or *alta* if rouge is unavailable), artificially converting the eyebrows to a uni-brow, and applying surma to their eyes, these residents of hell on earth have tried their best to conceal their ugliness, but in most cases this attempt to play god have been partly or totally unsuccessful. The men on the street, their eyes like Siva under intoxication, are looking skywards, doing their best to satiate the hunger of the eyes with the nectar of their beauty—someone is ridiculing these women by cracking really disgraceful jokes, someone else making a meaningful gesture from downstairs and wrapping a wrapper from head to mouth to hide his face is hurriedly entering the house, certain mischievous youngsters having thrown burning red or blue matchsticks at them are walking away laughing despite stomaching ugly abuse. And some others are not even deterred to throw firecrackers—multicolour matchsticks—into the balcony. Today the skies above the street are variegated and noisy with various kinds of fireworks and human voices while the air has the foul smell of gunpowder. From time to time the burnt remnants of a rocket is rushing down with speed and crashing with a thud on a pedestrian's head, startling him completely. To protect themselves from crashing fireworks, a few people are walking cautiously with umbrellas.

The ritual worship of Kartick and Saraswati is performed in many Calcutta homes, and these two deities are very dear to the prostitutes. But it's difficult to understand the reason behind this. Kartick is the commander of the armies of the gods, he has never married and his character is unblemished, how could he become dear to the prostitutes? By worshipping Kartick, perhaps the

prostitutes want to convey to us men the following thoughts—
'The wives are our main enemies, so don't ever get married and
instead worship us with devotion.' I won't be too surprised if this
theological explanation happens to be true. At least we have a
fictitious interpretation of the Kartick affinity of prostitutes but
why the embodiment of learning or *vidya* (Saraswati), happens
to be worshipped in the abodes of these creatures known as
*avidya*s—literally the absence of 'vidya'—is impossible to figure
out.

On the nights of the ritual worship of Kartick and Saraswati,
the prostitutes are richly benefitted from the cash gifts offered by
the babus, because they lovingly invite most of their paramours
and friends. A serious one-upmanship ensues between the
babus regarding the giving of cash—if one gives five rupees,
another would give ten, and seeing that another big-heart would
perhaps put down twenty. The prostitutes get more pleased
as the competitive spirit grows. Just as in the puja ceremonies
performed in respectable households, here too the arrangements
for entertaining and taking care of the guests are perfect to a
fault. The more punctilious among the invitees sit down in the
well decorated assembly room, leaning against pillows, and
taking a few drags from the silver encased hubble-bubble or
gorgora pipe and after having a *paan* or two, slip away on some
pretext, without partaking of the meal at the brothel. But still
there is never a dearth of decent folks at a place where food is
being served, in fact they are more in number. Would those, who
are prepared to squander away all their possessions at the feet of
a prostitute, be at all bothered about social norms? On the day
of the invitation the festivities continue till late into the night,

and the well-off prostitutes also make lots of arrangements for song, dance and entertainment for the pleasure of the guests. That day, liquor bottles empty at the blink of an eye. Sometimes, uncle and nephew having gone to the same house as invitees are caught red-handed by each other. Over and above this, clever prostitutes recover all expenses of the puja by cajoling the most soft-headed of their friends. Not so long ago, a youngish babu of the *subarnabanik* community made a big name for himself in this matter among the ranks of captains. That chap having hardly learnt to fly and squander his father's wealth, had spent five hundred or seven hundred for the making of a gorgeous Saraswati idol and on the night of the puja had recklessly spent proportionate sums of money on other things. And it didn't surprise me at all when some days later I heard this chap had filed for insolvency. This is because I know the weird psychology that drives these profligate captain-babus. Knowing that they will be roasted alive, still like insects they rush towards the fire, as if their joy is in a fiery death. Even when neck deep in debt, they try their best to sink deeper and wouldn't swim even if they knew how to. This too is a kind of madness or suicide, what else!

On the night of the Phooldol festival, a wonderful scene can be observed on Nimtala Street. Along this road one can find temples of numerous gods and goddesses, one beside the other. Small or big marquees are erected in front of most of these temples and thin carpets or *satranji*s and sheets are laid on the floor. Groups of people sitting around, play music and sing songs. Somewhere a group dressed like bauls, the mystic minstrels, dance as they sing. At another place *baithaki* songs, which are suited for assemblies or parties, are sung. Elsewhere various kinds of musical instruments can be heard being played. The programme of *baithaki* songs held at Nimtala's Anandamayee temple is the most famous. There, many well-known singers and musicians display or rather playout their individual skills that day. The audience is often unbidden or they are drawn by the sounds. But they are also warmly welcomed with *paan* and other consumables. Many prostitutes and young women from semi-decent families are seen on this street that night. The appreciative audience has their ears for the songs while resting their eyes on these women. These connoisseurs don't forget to follow these women at the right time.

In Calcutta neighbourhoods, the programmes surrounding occasional festivals are held in shared community spaces or the *barwaritala*. In this matter too, Pathureghata was counted as the top destination till a few years back. An idol of the dimensions of Pathureghata's Vindhyabasini has not been seen till date in any community puja. During immersion, it was not possible for people to carry this idol on their backs; it was placed in a long and wide carriage which was pulled along by hundreds. The idol when placed above the carriage was no less than two and half storeys high, it was a huge affair. Alongwith this there were also arrangements for *sawng*s—the pantomime jesters—enacting religious and other themed performances. The puja continued for three days, and every day and night the *barwaritala* reverberated with the sounds of the gigantic crowds assembled there to enjoy the best *jatra* or folk theatre, the devotional kirtan songs and more. Next to Vindhyabasini it is worth naming the community pujas of Lohapatti and Jorabagan. In both these places the deity is Rakshakali. The community performance by *sawng*s at

Lohapatti is very famous. There, during the community puja, the arrangements for *jatra* and other entertainments for the day, to be followed through the night, continues till date. The women in the audience of most of these community festivals include a large number of prostitutes of the lower categories.

There are many other kinds of festivities held in Calcutta at night. But it's not possible to provide a complete account here.

SCENE EIGHT
INHABITANTS OF THE UNDERWORLD

Winter night …

This winter is such a spoilsport; it doesn't respect the fancies of the babus. Throttling the south wind, spoiling the show of the fine powdery *ilsa-guri* drizzle—resembling the roe of the hilsa fish which thrives and breeds in the rains—striking a thunderous blow to Saturday merrymaking, a hoary winter sits firmly over the city, least bothering about the curses of the natives. Even a neighbourhood like Sonagachhi, always aglow with the light of beauty, seems to be seized by a stillness by the strike of nine in the night. At midnight there is not a single living soul to be spotted here. Burdened by ancient memories of the final resting place of some long gone *gaji*—a Muslim religious warrior— named Sona, Sonagaji or Sonagachhi named after him and now stupefied amidst the blurry silence of a blanketing fog, looks much like a cemetery. The *sakher-babu*s have carefully plugged every opening of their rooms and taken refuge under their quilts to 'boycott' the cold wind. Meanwhile the divine beauties of love preside as solitary goddesses over the domain of their empty rooms, preparing to light makeshift twig fires and exterminate the biting cold as the market for customer babus is out-of-reach for them tonight. Driven out of every home, winter rages through the streets of Calcutta, sighing deeply, exhaling a freezing, chilly breath—unleashing its fury on the poor.

The fog is deep, it is everywhere. Wherever I look there is only fog and smoke. The glowing brightness of Calcutta has been tarnished. Even the gas lights, wrapped in fog and smoke, stare weakly, like the teary lacklustre eyes of the wretched. Every door and window of the houses on both sides is shut—no signs of life are visible from the outside. From time to time a blustery wind rises, blowing from some snow-laden desert, its ice-cold gusts lashing onto that unfortunate soul, who was still out on the road as work was not over yet, almost freezing the blood in the veins. A shadowy sickle of a moon does hang in the sky but looks scrawny and deathly pale.

Hey you, the luxury-loving, lying in great comfort in your cosy bed! For a moment emerge from your night's warm covers and step outside. For a while, in this break from your pleasant dreams, have a look at the harsh face of reality. There is no joy in this but you will get an idea, how much suffering is bred from destiny's heartless laughter.

Look! There goes an old man holding the old woman's hand. He is broken and bent over. This old man is blind—he is being led by the dim vision of the old woman. He has no cloth covering his torso, and a torn loincloth hangs from his waist. With socks, shoes, sweater, comforter, waistcoat, coat, overcoat, ulster, one or two shawls and the raging fire of youth, you are still unable to tame this winter but this old man and woman, how do they keep alive in this biting cold? Shivering from cold, his teeth chattering noisily, the old man calls out endlessly in a doleful and piteously pleading tone—'Spare me a coin; Babu, spare me a coin!' You are nurtured and raised in the warmth of shawls, you pass by pushing him away … your pocket is full of silver coins…but the old couple won't get even a single one of those. But still they continue with their doleful cries. Despite having struggled against hopelessness all their lives, they haven't lost hope, despite having cried all their lives, the source of their tears haven't dried up, despite having offered prayers that went unanswered all their lives, their prayers haven't fallen silent. They are nothing but rejects of the world, influenza and pneumonia doesn't beckon them. They beckon those who have youth on their side, those for whom the world is a festive house, those whom the world loves.

Proceed a few more steps. Look at the bare footpaths on the sides of the street—rows of people are lying side by side—this winter, the fog and the chilling wind around them. They are homeless; they are born and they die on the streets. Sometimes a winter rain falls and then their cup of enjoyment is certainly brimful. There are dogs on the street, there are cats, but these are people, humans! People like you and me. Like you and me they are residents of the capital city. Like you and me, the subjects of the same king, children of the same god, moved by the same joys and sorrows. And still there is so much difference between them and us! This unimaginable misfortune of humanity is peculiar to Calcutta, the capital city. Such a sight is rare in the villages.

Keep moving, keep moving! One after the other, the scenes are changing right before our eyes. Look how the roadside eateries have been decorated. Their huge clay ovens alight with the big vent at the bottom—where the ash and cinder accumulate. Sometimes you will find the wretched, stricken with cold, having stuck both their feet inside these vents, sleeping like someone fatally injured, bereft of all senses. You and I won't be able to tolerate that heat but they don't feel it! Maybe, the skin singeing heat is more desirable for them rather than dying from the biting cold.

At the entrance and on the sides of dark and dirty gullies, low class prostitutes stand like statues of stone late into the night. Winter nights provide indisputable proof, how bereft of desire their flesh trade really is. When the night is deep, when streets are deserted, when the cold of the winter is biting, when the excruciatingly cold dew falls, when the pye-dogs have also vanished, they still stand on the street. There is no chance of a client coming, still they stand, pitting hope against hope. The fog and smoke choke them, still they stand—they freeze from the cold, the body refusing to take it anymore, still they stand. Four annas, six annas, eight annas, that too they don't make every day. From time to time the police come and these women run for their lives, hiding in their dwellings or holes which resemble the underworld. Cane strikes, slaps and heavy fists rain down on those unable to escape. After a while you notice they are back at their respective stations. Sometime ago, I had seen a saheb from the Jorabagan police barracks give chase to one of these unfortunate women. Within a short distance the saheb grabbed the fringe of her sari but without the slightest hesitation, the terror-stricken woman unwrapped her sari and threw away her clothes in one swift movement, running down the street stark naked. This was a scene, new to the sahib; he stood there, motionless with shock. Some women don't run away even on seeing the police guards; on the contrary, the guards banter with them in broken Bangla. The reason is nothing else—it's not a relationship of love! If you go through the guard's pocket you will find one or two hard-earned copper coins of this unfortunate woman, stored there with care. My eyes moisten on seeing them, they may be prostitutes but they are not inanimate. I'm told that when Vidyasagar came across women of this class while walking down the street, he would give a bit of money to each of them. His kind soul could not but respond to their sorrow. The police don't object when high class prostitutes set up the display of their sex trade on the verandah, but all their stubbornness is directed at these women. This is supposed to be illegal. Why isn't it illegal for prostitutes to stand on the verandah? Does the law apply only to the poor?

There are *paan* shops at every crossing. The numbers of women *paan* sellers are gradually increasing in these shops— under the garb of selling *paan*, their sex trade continues unabated. These shops are popular haunts for police guards. If the winter gets too harsh and the spirit begins to freeze over, the police guard, twirling his moustache and beard and wearing an amorous smile on his lips, proceeds towards the *paan* shop to warm up his damp and sagging spirit. The *paanwali* too, returning a sweet smile, immediately prepares one or two good *paan*s and presents these to the guard with Golapi beedis. Then they continue with their whispery love talk. Despite the amorous exchanges, the police guard doesn't get carried away, his eyes remain very alert—not to catch a thief but wary, that some superior might suddenly turn up. The *paanwali*s of Calcutta streets are to a police guard like an oasis in the desert—a tiny drop of joy in the midst of great sorrow.

On winter nights, poor Biharis, the residents of the neighbouring state of Bihar who had migrated to the city in search of jobs, light big fires at certain street crossings and sit in circles around these. After a day's hard labour the night brings them some respite, and they don't want to perish, shivering in the cold. They break out in a chorus while warming themselves by the flames—dhols and *kartal*s accompanying the singing, gradually the singing and the music rising to a crescendo, and by and by turning into a meaningless din. Due to these *khachmach, dumdaam, hoichoi* noise, sleep is driven away—disappearing completely from everyone's eyes in the neighbourhood—the rich of the area turn crimson with rage. The music continues unabated late into the night, till the time fingers go slack and the voice gets tired. It's not possible for us to comprehend the element of enjoyment in all this. The poor best know what they do enjoy.

Ever been to a *bhikiripara*, the beggars' quarters? There are *bhikiripara*s in parts of Calcutta but most of us don't know that these exist. Here live those who survive on the charity of others. This is what distinguishes them from ordinary people and because of this difference their characters don't match with the rest of us. Many of us knowingly maintain a relationship with thieves, cheats, and dishonest people of society, but no one is prepared to fraternise with beggars, this despite the fact that there are always many beggars in gentleman's garb in our midst. Those who have taken to begging as a public profession may be excluded from society at large but they do have their own social life. There is no similarity between that way of life and the rules and strictures of the *Manu Samhita*. From time to time I have peeped into the life of *bhikiripara*. The narratives of their joys and suffering could have added a new dimension to Bengali literature but unlike Russia no Bengali Maxim Gorky has been born in this country. So we cannot find any mind-boggling depiction of this society of socially excluded people in our literary outpourings.

There is not much to see during the day in a *bhikiripara*. This is because at this time the inhabitants visit different parts of Calcutta for their daily trade. Also with the coming of night many do not return—the lame and the blind fake beggars are among this group. Those who pretend to be blind despite having good eyes cannot make much in the daytime. This is because the almsgivers have good eyes, they are not blind. It is worth watching the gathering of beggars at dusk. Usually beggars live in the most scruffy and inferior neighbourhoods—the *bhikiripara* of the city. Narrow gullies, hardly any light or clean air coming through, dirt and garbage strewn around and in the midst of this, in leaning mud houses with clay tiled roofs, live the beggars. Many of them are hereditary beggars—they have been in the same trade for generations. Examples of a pauper's son becoming king in good time, are not rare. But perhaps, one born of a blood nourished from begging can never earn a name as a worker. So a beggar's son has to be a beggar—an incompetent, scrounger—laziness is such a familial illness. And how can I call it laziness—the labour of those employed in a job is much easier compared to the amount of mental and physical labour they have to put in to collect alms. And yet they are unable to work at a proper job, attachment to begging is in their veins. It's like an addiction for opium or cocaine, once habituated, there's no way out.

Many beggars live with their families—their mother, sister, wife, son, and daughter are all beggars. Though they may be

Hindus by religious persuasion, they are not strict casteists. I have seen certain beggars who have married the lowest class of prostitutes or their daughters. Here, character has little or no value. No one will have anything to say if a beggar's wife or daughter publicly adopts prostitution as a profession. They are least bothered by any social norms—their sole purpose is to keep body and soul together by any means whatsoever.

Inside their small hole-like rooms on some lane, the adda or idle talk among young beggars gets quite lively. Earlier, a young beggar used to come to my house. He was called 'Pagla'— the mad one—by everybody. His daily takings, from singing songs, were not negligible. By striking up a friendship with this Pagla, I had visited and spent time at the hovels—the dwelling places of beggars—two or three times. On the first occasion, my appearance in their hovel in the midst of their adda, left them all dumbstruck. They scrutinised my face repeatedly with a lot of suspicion and astonishment. Some of them tried to run away, perhaps suspecting me to be a policeman. These people are very scared of the police. This is because, while out begging, they don't hesitate to steal small utensils and possessions from the homes of common folk.

But Pagla told them reassuringly, 'Fear not brother … fear not. This babu is known to me, he has come to see our hovel. You have fun, babu will tip you generously when he leaves.'

While their astonishment about my strange fancy did not diminish it was clear from their faces that they felt somewhat reassured.

The room had mud-splattered uneven walls, and the lower half of the wall facing the street had its skeletal split-bamboo frame exposed by the lashing rain. Higher up, the walls were adorned with pictures from calendars and advertisements of cheap cigarettes. On one side was a bare plank bed covered by a tattered mat with a couple of dirty oil-stained pillows without pillowcases. The pillows were so dirty that from a casual glance they seemed to be made from 'oil-cloth'. On another side, two split bamboo frames were laid out on the mud floor. In one corner was a portable clay oven and some metal pots stacked one on top of the other. I understood that this same room turns into a sitting-room, kitchen or bedroom as and when required.

The men in the room were either lying down or sitting around in groups, some on the floor, others on the bed. They looked scruffy like scarecrows. God only knows how many days some of them hadn't taken a bath. The clothes they wore were dirty, torn or patched up. The room has such a mixed stench that my nose began to trouble me very soon. And above that was the smell of marijuana smoke. A clay pipe was being passed around through almost every hand. A man, skinny like a lizard, was leaning against the wall. He was holding a small hookah with a long stem. In a while he took a drag from the pipe and a little spark leapt out of his hookah. This one was a *gulikhor*, an opium smoker. Another thin man took out a small wrapper from the folds of his cloth and opening it wide before his mouth carefully licked up a white powdery substance. This one was a cocaine user. After a while a woman entered the room. I guess she wouldn't be more than twenty-four or twenty-five but she had become so gaunt that one could call her old. She had a jet-black complexion and it seemed that what she wore had been printed in the same colour. She had not a bit of shyness amongst this roomful of men, and that she was a woman in their midst—apparent from the fact that the twin signs of womanhood on her chest were completely bare and visible.

Seeing her, someone inside the room said, 'Hey Potlir-Ma, what brings you here?'

'Well Bishe, do you have a *puriya* or something?'

'Hmm, got two maybe. Why do you ask?'

'Bro give me one please,' Potli's mother said.

'By Mary! What will I have if my stock gets depleted?'

'I beg of you, dear. I am paying you. I will die if you don't give ... you wish that?'

'Why, if you have run out of *puriya*s, go to Algu's adda?'

'You think I didn't? The adda is closed. Heard the police had been there.'

'Oh! Adda closed! Then if I give you a *puriya* who will take care of me,' Bishe rolled his eyes and exclaimed.

'So you won't give, right?'

Bishe shook his head furiously communicating his refusal!

'I see, you scraggy critter of a man, I will remember this. Next time when you are short of stock and fall at my feet, I will pay you back with the whack of a stick,' Potli's mother was going to say something more but Pagla warned her,

'Shut up Potlir ma, can't you see babu sitting in here!'

Finally Potli's mother's eyes fell on me. She stared, dumbstruck for a moment, then quickly covering up her breasts, left the room. So she did have some little sense of modesty!

'By the way, Pagla, what was Potli's ma asking for?' I said.

'Babu, she has run out of cocaine, so she came here in desperation ... and what kind of man are you Bishe! You saw

Potlir-Ma genuinely suffering, what would it matter to you if you gave her a *puriya*?'

'What do you mean, mate! And after that? At whose feet would I beg for it? You heard Algu's adda is closed.'

'You should still have given a *puriya*.'

'No, I haven't given and won't, it's my wish,' Bishe sounded annoyed! 'Only the other day you bought a pint of booze, did you share even a drop with me? Look at yourself before giving sermons.'

Pagla threw me a furtive glance and looked quickly away, continuing to sit with awkward embarrassment writ large on his face; I was now aware of the fact that he drank.

This is a partial depiction of the beggars of Calcutta. These are the groups of indigent destitute beggars whose grief-stricken faces, doleful looks, and distressed voices melt our hearts and minds. We give them alms. But that money is used for the worship of addiction. There are certain other houses in Calcutta belonging to the rich and the opulent—and not just in the house of the wealthy Rajen Mullick—where beggars are fed daily meals. Most of them have their meals there while putting away our donations for purchasing liquor, ganja, charas, *guli* or cocaine. Therefore it is us who bear the costs of their addiction. And like this, sitting on the lowest tiers of the dark underworld of degeneration, they continue to pass their days of an animal existence.

There is much more variety in Calcutta's underworld. The word 'underworld' used in the title of this chapter and rather appropriately coined by the English is present in its truest sense in the depravity of the dark hell hole where the residents are thieves, dacoits, murderers and the indigent from the lower classes. Among the lower classes and the poor, poverty is always the precursor of sin.

One night at around three o' clock, I was passing through Jorabagan on my way back. There was a friend with me, a well-known man of letters.

Suddenly from the side of a street we heard many voices and the sounds of song, dance and music. There was a gully right there. Beside it was an open plot of land where a marquee had been put up. Advancing a few steps and peeping inside, we found a large festive gathering. A *baiji*—a female professional singer and dancer—was singing and about a hundred and fifty people were sitting and listening. Almost all the listeners hailed from regions west of Bengal—bordering the 'up country'—and most of them drove bullock carts. They drove cattle carts by day and turned gangsters by night. Most Calcuttans didn't know how dangerous these cart drivers were. Right in front of my eyes, I've seen them beating up and robbing pedestrians. Many notorious criminals of Calcutta are carters or owners of bullock-cart sheds. Not very long ago near Nimtala ghat, right next to the Jorabagan police court, these goondas raided a country-liquor shop in broad daylight, demanding free drinks. When the owners refused, they murdered one and left two others grievously injured. But the English law is so complicated that despite being arrested they didn't get punished.

So such murderers and professional strongmen who beat up their victims do have fancies! It was amazing how, pretending to be gentle folk, they were listening to the songs of the *baiji* tonight. I was seized by a sudden fancy to go uninvited and sit in the midst of their festive gathering to study their attitudes, and observe their gestures for a while. I revealed my secret wish to my friend, he was completely against it.

'What are you saying, are you out of your mind! Knowingly offer oneself for slaughter! Never!'

Perhaps it was Bankimchandra who had once said, 'Certain young boys instead of being frightened when told about the bugbear want to see it.' From a young age my nature is quite like this. Because of it, I have been in danger many times, but the new experience I gathered from these dangerous situations, and the opportunity they provided for me to observe the astonishing variety of human nature and character, are rare in the life of the common Bengali. Life—I wished to observe life. It's not possible to do this while lying in bed or reading fancy books.

Assuring my friend, I said, 'Fear not! Let's go in with Goddess Durga's blessings and Her name on our lips. You will see there will be no trouble.'

I knew goondas quite well. However dangerous their exteriors might look, at the bottom of their hearts they were not exactly like that. If required they could very easily snuff out someone's life but that is their trade, and that ruthlessness is temporary. In their day-to-day existence, they are just people like you and me. And then, just like we do, they love, they show affection and indulge in merry-making. Also, they are not bereft of the religion of kindness. I know a ruthless goonda called Mahadeo—I've often seen him giving alms to the lame or blind. In friendship too they are more worthy than many gentlemen. They can smilingly sacrifice their lives for someone they know to be a friend. And they won't let a fly hurt those who, trusting them, seek their shelter. There are uncountable numbers of goondas in the Calcutta neighbourhood where I live. So I had the opportunity to study their characters inside out. No human being is totally bad.

I was certain that when goondas are indulging in pleasure, they wouldn't even think of trouble. Especially when we have consciously arrived in their dominion, surrendering ourselves to their trust. They would definitely preserve the dignity borne out of our dependence on them. Therefore, dragging my friend along, and jumping across a bamboo fence, I went and sat right in the middle of that festive gathering.

They kept watching our faces with great astonishment. Perhaps they were finding it unbelievable that two innocent and decent-looking persons could come uninvited, so late in the night, and sit in the midst of their festive gathering. But very soon they took our sudden appearance quite easily. A few men respectfully shifted away, making enough space around us so that we didn't face any discomfort in the closely crammed crowd. Then the singing, dancing and music continued unfettered—no one even asked who we are, why we had arrived there so late in the night? This was as I had expected—I hadn't misread their characters.

Both the *baiji*s were Bengali and one of them was quite good-looking. They were singing well too. These people have taste. With every new song the tabla and *baya* were changing hands—the number of instrumentalists among them was not few. They have learned not only to wield the dagger but I find they do cultivate the arts. In fact, each of them was playing the music very well. It's rare to find so many skilled players even amongst the festive gatherings of gentlefolk.

From the attitude and demeanour of the *baijis*, I felt that they were quite pleased to see us in the midst of these hordes of unsightly looking men from distant provinces. Before noticing us they had their backs turned in our direction but later, they sat facing us and began singing again. Both of them were covered with jewellery—they hadn't reckoned while accepting the booking amount that they would have to enter the tiger's den tonight. They were obviously inwardly scared but for no good reason. The tigers only wanted to play tonight, they didn't have an eye on the jewellery.

Truly, this was a very perceptive audience. They were sitting quietly, rapt in attention, drinking in the nectar of music and applauding on the right occasions. I hadn't come across such a perceptive audience ever before, even among the festive gatherings of gentlefolk. I had been to musical programmes in country houses of the rich and the wealthy ... what a hubbub, what revelry ... would one dare make enlivening music there? The real reason behind such merriment is alcohol. But even though the glory of the goddess of spirits was absent here it didn't take a while to make out, by observing the faces, that most people in the audience were steeped in intoxication from bhang.

A little while later some men came over and insisted that we be their guests for dinner—this was special treatment indeed, almost deserving of an adored son-in-law. After much effort we convinced them that we were not habituated to having a meal at four in the morning, that we had had dinner at home and so on. Then we left. This was because it was clear from my friend's face that despite receiving such care and attention, he wasn't feeling reassured—he was feeling like a fish out of water. So this was our experience of hearing *baiji*s sing in a goondas' den. I guess you have by now realised that Satan is not as dark as he is depicted in the pictures.

SCENE NINE

PLAYHOUSE

Previously we used to spend nights at folk theatre shows or jatra, now the time for leisure is spent at theatre halls. It can be said that the educated Bengali has more or less 'boycotted' jatras and the jatra performers groups—jatra parties are gradually disappearing under the sway of numerous professional and amateur theatre groups. So, in an effort towards self-preservation, the managers of jatra parties have nowadays taken to emulating theatre. The 'theatrical jatra parties' of this day are evidence of this fact. This has resulted in form-related changes of the jatra, a change in style of acting, a change in the tunes of the songs, and often public playhouses of Calcutta are taken on rent for these jatra performances. In fact these are neither jatra nor theatre.

When we were young we used to watch jatra in the houses where Durga Pujo was held or in community spaces, till late into the night. One still remembers what a painful experience it used to be. Western civilisation has a detached aloofness about it—in meetings and gatherings everyone has to have a separate seat of their own. But in eastern civilisations we find an obtrusive over zealousness. At home, large joint families are always at pains to resolve all issues of disunity and outside too, in meetings and gatherings, everyone is packed close to each other sharing a common seating area. I am not going to discuss here which system is beneficial but I do remember what terrible discomforts we had to bear at the jatra performances in summer. A huge crowd would have gathered in a small space on a hot and muggy night, we would be getting soaked from head to toe from the flowing sweat, those days electric fans whirring above were beyond our imagination, and there was not a hair's breadth of space left for movement because from left, right, front and back, crowds of people seemed to be pressing at us with all their might. Many of them stank horribly, many were elbowing, and many were doing whatever other things, thinking of which still gives me the shivers. Right then, Bidyasundar's Malini, unshaved and with a bristling beard, saying, 'How do I provide flowers for the king's palace every day,' sometimes clapping like a hijra or transgender, sometimes pulling up the dress a little above the knees exposing rough black legs, danced around the stage and left; Bidya's mother would begin to wail; the king and the chief guard roared threateningly; swarthy potbellied youngsters dressed like maidens, wearing damaged wigs of unruly dry tresses, would sing in absurd tones assaulting our ears; the chorus dressed in long flowing lawyers' robes standing in the four corners would strike and jab powerfully as if fist-fighting with an invisible enemy, while making chilling facial contortions and bleating goat-like in their effort to ornament the *taan*—a fast trill of notes—and in the process would be performing the last rites of Tansen, the legendary musician.

We did not forget to applaud as we sat stiff and wide-eyed, watching these blurry scenes, in the dim glow of chandeliers till the early hours before dawn. Then the performance would be over and many of us would be unable to find their shoes. When we returned home, tired of body and mind, we felt we had been wrestling all through the night. I am aware that jatra is pure and indigenous but from what we had viewed and experienced in our childhood, I am constrained to say that it is a terribly home grown or swadeshi, affair. And it is perhaps because of this that people nowadays, forsaking free jatra performances, prefer to spend money from their pockets to watch the theatre.

Theatre is a most noteworthy destination of Calcutta's nights. There are an endless number of theatre lovers among the residents of Calcutta. Here at the theatre, our national characteristics stand out very prominently before our eyes and ears.

While Bengalis have indeed established theatres in this country following in the footsteps of the sahebs, most of the desirable traits of English theatre are not to be found in Bengali playhouses. Leave alone England or Europe, a visit to the English theatres of Calcutta (Empire Theatre for example) is a feast for the eyes. It is a huge four-storied building with a marble encased staircase leading all the way up right from the ground floor to the second floor. There is nowhere an excess of ornamentation to trouble finer tastes, on the contrary simple clean aesthetics captivate the mind. Such a large building, so many people passing through each day and yet so sparkling clean and tidy that even with a microscope it might be impossible to find a speck of dirt or refuse. I will try to discuss at an appropriate place what a pitiable state, compared to these English theatres, are the playhouses in which Bengalis spend night after night.

There is not the slightest sign of poverty or distress peering out from inside the English playhouses. The viewers come here and pay money to spend the night joyfully amidst aesthetically pleasing surroundings. Knowing this, the owners of these English theatres don't provide spurious products in exchange for good money. Here the backdrops don't display any evidence of unsure hands wielding the brush, no showiness nor the use of incongruous colours that would please a child, no inopportuneness, no unnaturalness and no inconsistency. But a glance at Bengali playhouses will reveal ugly wooden or bamboo frames, ropes and torn pieces of cloth peering at us from the ceiling, no resemblance between the wings and the backdrop, tattered and discoloured backdrops painted ages ago patched in with new ones, bare and dusty planks of wood visible below the stage and similar errors and omissions in the costumes of the actors.

Even in the matter of acting there is a similar divergence between English actors and the locals or desi. It can be well said that those actors who usually perform in the Calcutta playhouses of the sahebs are minor players in the community of actors of England. But even these minors could be gurus to most of our top-ranked actors. They may be minor in England but the amount of arduous practice they put in to present an engrossing performance, is perhaps not attempted by Bengali actors even in their dreams. At least this is what one begins to suspect after watching their performances and those of ours. The difference between the complete and the incomplete, the seasoned and the novice, the prepared and the unprepared, is exactly of the same order. The main reason behind this is that English actors first take lessons at acting school, then after days of gathering experience through apprenticeship at playhouses they get the opportunity to appear on stage with a significant role. Supposedly, the actors of our country need no training in acting, it's as if they are actors by birth. Secondly the duration of rehearsal-time in desi playhouses is so minimal that fine acting is completely impossible. I know of plays being staged before the public after only two or three days of rehearsals. But let's leave this topic for now because we are not here for theatre criticism. I just gave a couple of hints in trying to explain the kind of cheating the Bengali audience exposes themselves to, while spending money and sitting up nights.

Our playhouses provide many cunning youngsters the opportunity to cheat their parents. When they just about take wings, these youngsters visit brothels while telling their parents they are 'going to watch a theatre'. Many of them somehow get hold of the printed theatre programme. If their fathers or mothers express any kind of suspicion, they present the programme to prove that they are speaking the truth. Even when returning late at night, the only plea is, 'been to the theatre'. Most parents are so simple-minded that they are satisfied by this answer. Actually they should spell out in clear terms that young boys won't be allowed to visit the theatre without a guardian. This will defeat their designs. At this early stage, youngsters are cowardly. There is still time to reform many of them if they can be restrained at this age. Later when they become habitual visitors to brothels, their hearts go up in flames. Then it's impossible to get them back.

Many come to watch the theatre as escorts of women. Sending the women upstairs they slip away from the theatre hall. Then spending their time outside in merry-making they return a little before the show gets over to collect the women and return home. But it's impossible for anyone to find out what transpires secretly in between. Yet at times these extra clever types also get caught red-handed. The show is over, all the women have come down, but the women from a certain house are still sitting silently and waiting, because their escort has not turned up. Gradually the night gets deeper and the women begin to cry out of fear. Just then, the protector might be sitting somewhere enjoying a *khemta* dance. Maybe he has lost the count of time after having downed two glasses on the request of his friends. Then suddenly he comes to his senses on hearing the clock strike three in the night....

With much reluctance I am forced to mention another incident here. Our book will remain incomplete if we always try to be guarded and draw a veil over these stories of nighttime scandals ... everyone should know that the following account is completely true, only the names of the hero and heroine are imaginary.

Amala is a widow, young and beautiful. She is not devoid of any of the talents which make the ideal heroine of a contemporary novel.

The life of young widows in this country is considered to be the substance of tragedy. Amala's life could have been the same but Jatishchandra, who lived next door, saved her from that terrible predicament, albeit in complete secrecy. I guess these words do not need any further elucidation.

There is a very narrow lane next to the room where Amala sleeps. Jatish's house is right on the other side. They see each other every day through the windows of their rooms. But that's the end of the matter. Amala's folks are very alert, they are unable to appreciate the worthiness of love.

But the God of love, Madanthakur, is much more powerful and intelligent than Amala's folks. Because of his divine grace a path is cut, even through an impenetrable forest of thorny nettles, away from everyone's eye. Therefore …

One day Jatish tied a letter to a string and hung it from his roof right into Amala's room. Amala read it. I don't know what was written in that letter. But after reading it, Amala smiled and nodded, communicating her agreement.

Amala's folks often go to the theatres, cannot say whether they buy tickets or get passes. Right the next day after getting the letter, Amala went to watch a play, alone except for her brother-in-law as an escort. Her brother-in-law was also a passionate admirer of the theatre. She often went to watch plays accompanied by him. It was not possible for other members of the household to go every time she went. Sending Amala upstairs, Amala's brother-in-law bought his ticket and went inside.

The play had just begun when a female attendant came up to Amala and said, 'A certain babu of a certain address is calling you.' The attendant mentioned her brother-in-law's name as a reference.

Coming out onto the street Amala found a car waiting, Jatish was inside. She boarded the car without uttering a word. After driving around different streets for two hours the car returned to the gates of the theatre hall. Amala quietly walked into the theatre hall.

Who could vouch for the fact that many such incidents did not occur at the theatre hall? We have heard several other rumours but I am not going into those because I cannot swear on their veracity. One cannot say whether female attendants of theatre halls are involved in these goings-on. At least one doesn't have any evidence to support this.

The theatre cannot be blamed for such transgressions. This sinful playacting won't come to an end even if theatres are abolished. It will only find other ways of expression.

The playhouse happens to be the confluence of three streams of fine arts. Whatever is enjoyable in literature, music and painting should come together in the playhouse. If the eyes, the ears and the mind suffer pain instead of getting enchanted by this place, then one would understand that the playhouse has failed to hold on to its ideals. But let us now have a look at what the eyes, the ears and the mind have to really suffer on a visit to a Bengali theatre.

First of all let us have a look at the scene right outside the Bengali theatres. The exteriors of arts and culture venues should be gorgeous and the owners of our playhouses do understand that. This is why there was an effort to focus on architectural splendour in the design of Star, the recently shutdown Minerva and other theatres. Even a truly beautiful Calcutta building like Star Theatre, because of a lack of finer taste of the owners and the influence of the money making ideal, grievously hurts the eyes. Why are ugly looking *paan*-beedi shops allowed to be set up next to theatre halls or within the premises? It is very wrong to sully the beauty and appeal of these palatial mansions built with so much care, labour, and expenditure for just a few rupees of rent— this only suits a dyed-in-the-wool business community member from another part of the country. For Bengalis, who are at the forefront in the cultivation of fine arts in modern India, this is an unpardonable offence.

The interiors of the Bengali theatres come next. Here the distinguishing characteristics are dust, dirt, garbage, grime, filaments of soot, *paan* spittle and an unbearable stink.

Everywhere one looks, above or below, this side or that, one is bound to notice signs of the owner's negligence and at least one blemish or the other. There are frescoes on the ceiling, walls, and in front of the theatre stage. The expense incurred in getting these painted is not small, but it seems these fresco artists come from Barobazaar because one can never discern any artistic finesse or a distinctive style. Here you have layers upon layers of colours, you have a variety of leaves, vines and flowers, you have fairies with open wings and nude female forms, and you have much more of unintelligible scrawls and scratches, but there is no way to comprehend what ideal they follow. Somewhere we notice the ideals of Ajanta frescoes, elsewhere Egyptian or Mughal or English or the artist's own ideal which is devoid of any ideals at all. The audience from Hatkhola, without an ability to judge good from bad, might well gape with open-mouthed wonder at this silent delirium of art but it is not only Hatkhola from where Bengali theatre draws its audience. Here, the refined taste of this other audience is murdered by strangulation! The really lamentable fact is that that there is much evidence of our assertions in every theatre run by educated individuals and those of refined taste. Is it possible that the tastes of the educated get affected once they associate with the theatre?

Another speciality of Bengali theatres is the clamour of the audience. Such clamour is not even heard in Notun Bazaar. Sometimes, even during a performance, members of the audience keep shouting so loudly that the acting has to stop. During the interval between acts, the indefatigable clamour rises threefold, deafening ears. The authorities know best what strange logic persuades them to allow *paanwallas* inside the theatre hall. It is a terrible nuisance; they run back and forth continuously; and stepping on every toe, they will cry out 'paan-cigarette', and they will open soda bottles with loud pops placing them right next to your head. How irritating! The merciless affair which goes by the name of 'concert', present in most theatres, is nothing more than mechanical commotion. Perhaps even the beats of the *dhaak*, right next to our ears, would sound sweeter. Compared to all this, English theatres run by the sahebs are like a peaceful paradise. There the audience is also polite, and the orchestra music is an enjoyable experience.

Next the seating arrangements. There is neither an aisle for coming and going, like we find in an English theatre, nor the space between two rows is adequate. So when one person comes in or goes out, the situation of every other person in that row becomes absolutely miserable. (Nowadays the seating arrangements have improved a lot.) Besides this, every seat is so dirty, unsightly, and riddled with bedbugs that without being versed in *hatha yoga* it would be impossible to derive unperturbed pleasure from the performance for an extended period of time.

That we do not fret about visiting such a terrible place night after night to watch plays being performed ... does it leave any doubt about the fact that we are a first-rate theatre-loving people? There have been instances when starting from two in the afternoon the performance has continued till daybreak, and despite having watched it, this old heart continues to keep the beat. Under English law suicide is a punishable offence. Following this legal norm, a rule has been framed which prevents Bengalis from committing suicide by watching these relentless and life-threatening performances. It is now forbidden to continue

performances after one o' clock at night. But one can't say that this
law is being respected. For sure the government has appointed
inspectors but still, the enthusiasm for acting often does not cool
down in the Bengali theatres before it's about half past two or
three in the night. What does this imply? And then, the tendencies
of the Bengali audience are still partial towards shows going on till
late into the night. So whenever theatre authorities get a chance
they organise night long shows during festivals or by obtaining
special permission, and immediately hordes of audience head for
the theatre at breakneck speed.

The general scene during a performance in a Bengali theatre
is more or less like this—

The concert stops, relieving the auditory faculties of the
audience. A historical play is being staged. The performance
was to begin at seven but now it is eight already. Perhaps there
would have been further delay but agitated by incessant whistles
and clapping from the audience in the pit and the galleries, the
authorities are finally forced to raise the curtain. At the beginning
of the first scene one can see about twenty to twenty-five *sakhi*s or
female confidantes who range in age from ten to fifty and maybe
even more. They are standing, sitting or lying down in different
poses. Their faces are extremely red and extremely white from
the use of paint and powder. Same for their hands and feet. But
their real complexion is visible at the back of their heads, below
the hair buns. This part being invisible in the mirror, could not
be painted. Most of the *sakhi*s are either reed-thin or lardy and
fat. Not a single one of them have attractive faces or figures—
most have sunken beady eyes, blunt noses, and their cheeks were
sagging inwards. A flute, piano, tabla and harmonium begin to

play backstage and immediately this group of lightweights and heavyweights begin to sing and dance energetically in a style neither Indian or western. As a result of their noisy romping and jumping about, the dust of ages that had accumulated on the stage rose in clouds and attacked the viewers in the first few rows with a deadly valour. The viewers, sneezing loudly and coughing violently, firmly pressed handkerchiefs or the ends of their dhoti into their nostrils. The *sakhi*s, breathless after all the singing and dancing, were about to leave when the audience from the back clapped and shouted—'Encore! Encore!' But the viewers at the front, covered with dust, began to say, 'No more! No more!' So a fierce duel between 'encore' and 'no more' continues for some time. Meanwhile the *sakhi*s having caught their breath and rested a bit, returned on stage and left after another song and dance act. During the song and dance, a variety of vulgar or hilarious shouts and comments were heard from the gallery, all of which cannot be mentioned here. Just a few examples—'*bba-bba-bba-bba-bba-bba-bba-bba-bba!*'—'va-va-voom!', '*Le halua*', '*More jai, more jai*'—'Ohh, I'm dying, perishing', '*O, hohhoh!*', '*Pran je jae re baap*'—'My heart's going to stop!', '*Jaash ne bhai, amadero shonge niye ja*'—'Don't leave yet, dear, take us along!' etcetera.

In the first row of the playhouse sat some young dudes who were human versions of fan-tailed pigeons, they can be called popinjays. Most of them had the hair at the back of their heads shaved, quite probably with a Kropp razor, while at the front they had a knotted tuft—really the signs of branded convicts. The scent of 'honey' wafted from their breath and a liquor flask peeped out from the pocket of someone's churidar-punjabi. Each had their gaze fixed on the movements of different but particular dancers. The women too, while they danced, cast meaningful looks and smiled coyly at a fan-tailed pigeon each. It doesn't take time to understand that they know each other. As soon as the theatre is over their acquaintances will be deepened in some other location.

Up in the box seats the scene was equally strange. A group of babus sat in one of the boxes. Some of them beckoned the guard and placing a rupee or two in his hand, secretly found out the addresses of certain *sakhi*s, and whether they were 'taken' (booked) already. A bespectacled babu with a goatee was not watching the play at all—he stared transfixed at the second floor womens' seating area.

In the next box a group of Marwaris, sitting with one of the most famous beauties of Calcutta, attracted looks of hate and aversion from many Bengali *sakher-babu*s. Some of these babus were not deterred from screaming at and abusing them at the top of their voices, 'Because of the mischief of this *chhatu*-eating lot, we find the best of our bibis disappearing!' Despite getting abused in this manner, the Marwaris did not reveal any sign of irritation. Instead they smiled and gloated with boastful nonchalance.

In the next box with beds there were two babus and two bibis. One of the babus lay with his head on a bibi's lap. He had been brought down by an excess of spirits. The bibi affectionately caressed his hair. The second babu with a glass of liquor pleaded with the second bibi to take a sip of that drink.

The bibi pushed away the babu's hand carrying the glass saying, 'Go to hell, blackface! How can I drink in this bazaar—in front of so many people?'

The babu replied, 'You won't drink? Then I will kill myself.'

In the box right next to them, four gentlewomen, watching the drunken man beside them and overhearing these bawdy conversations broke into a cold sweat from fear and sat awkwardly stiff.

Meanwhile Nur Jahan and Sher Khan appear on stage engaged in romantic conversation. Upon seeing Nur Jahan, a loud uproar signifying inarticulate despair, rang through the hall. There was indeed reason for despair. Could this really be the world's most beautiful, the incomparable Nur Jahan. A forehead slightly smaller than the Garher Maath—the huge empty fields of the esplanade—with a parrot-like nose, bulbous meaty cheeks hanging on either side, an ear to ear smile, a folded chin, a pendulous belly, an elephantine body—how terrible! Even a caricature of Nur Jahan would be more presentable. All thanks to the unparalleled taste and amazing courage of the theatre authority. A member of the gallery audience unable to resist himself, shouted out loud—'Where exactly does this Nur Jahan reside, huh? Is it Sheoratola of Masjidbari?'

'*Eio*! Hey you, shut up!' the chief guard shouted and springing up from his seat, glared at the gallery seats. 'Who said that? Who said that?' he went on repeating.

But the chief guard's voice was helplessly drowned in the laughter and jeering of the whole audience.

Meanwhile a member of the audience, his mouth full of masticated *paan*, sneezed. A terrifying sneeze it was. Immediately, the head, shoulders, shawl and the shirt of the man right in front of him became strangely variegated with bits of *paan* leaves, betel nuts and red *paan* spittle. For a while this second member of the audience observed his own condition silently and with astonished eyes, then springing up from his seat, turned round and screamed, 'Now, tell me what is this!'

First man: (Wiping his face solemnly) 'I sneezed, couldn't hold it—what else?'

Second man: (Angrily) 'What else, want to see what else—you rascal!'

First man: (Standing up) 'What? Mind your tongue!'

Second man: 'You couldn't control your sneezing and I will control my words, stupid!'

First man: (Making a fist) 'Abusing again!'

Second man: (Suddenly punching the first man in the face) 'Damn, swine, donkey!'

The guards come running and grabbing them, take them outside—their tireless shouts continued to be heard from there.

After all this while, having finally got the opportunity to act, Nur Jahan began a romantic conversation with Sher Khan. But hardly a few words had been uttered, when from the upstairs ladies' seats, someone's infant child broke into an ear-piercing wail—'Whaaa'.

The male audience, sitting in the lower level, began to scream, 'For god's sake, calm down that baby, calm that baby down.'

Like mute wooden dolls, Nur Jahan and Sher Khan kept looking despondently upwards.

The bawling baby's cries became shriller. A woman could be heard saying in a peevish voice, 'What bother! Why don't you stop your son please?'

'Am I pinching him to make him cry? He is not stopping. What can I do?' The boy's mother retorted.

'What else? Go outside and calm him down.'

'Oh, I have to go outside! Why, haven't I paid a price for watching the show?'

And a womanly quarrel ensued. Right then something else was happening in another part of the theatre hall. A suspiciously foul-smelling stream of water had begun to rain down on the audience of a box which was right below the ladies seats— obviously another child's doing. New trouble broke out there too. So the acting now continued in the audience area while Sher Khan and Nur Jahan became the audience.

Come, let's now peer into the innards of the playhouse. For most of the audience sitting outside, the innards of a theatre is akin to some mysterious paradise. Bevies of divine beauties or *apsara*—Urvashis, Menokas and Rambhas—are said to roam about here. Many would perhaps be driven insane by a rush of joy if for once they were provided the opportunity to enter this paradise. Come, let me bestow upon you that rare fortune today.

But it's good to mention beforehand that on entering this place, many pleasant dreams, struck by the harshness of reality, would be shattered to smithereens.

On first entering the backstage area of most playhouses, the eyes will be hurt by a joyless scene of clutter, akin to a terribly messy godown. Countless blank backdrops are stacked side by side at one corner, bunches and coils of ropes and twines hang loose from another, torn cloth and dresses are piled high, elsewhere large rats run amok among a variety of stage props. Narrow passages run serpentine in every direction down which groups of people come and go bumping against each other. Air and light are forbidden there. You begin to feel suffocated simply standing there just for two minutes, and above all a mixed, rancid smell of cigarettes, tobacco, paint, glue, sweaty clothes and damp triggers a nauseous feeling. There is not a hint of 'paradise' in the backstage of a playhouse.

Around us are cell-like rooms—these are for those inhabitants of paradise who are of a comparatively higher social standing. On another side are two larger rooms. Dresses and costumes of many colours hang from ropes and clothes-horses inside. On the walls of each room is a large mirror. Inside the rooms are some tables, weathered from long use. Paint, paint bowls, mirrors, combs, brushes, powder, rouge, eyebrow pencils, wigs, false beards and moustaches, cigarette stubs, bits of food, glasses, chipped teacups, and several other things are scattered on the tables; here and there are stools or chairs with broken backrests; on the floor a host of Indian and foreign footwear, and at one corner of the room many fake spears, lathis, guns or swords—none of which is shiny; on the wall are a shield and brass anklets and so many other things, it's not possible to name them all. These two are the common dressing rooms—one for men and the other for women.

On another side of the stage there is a somewhat wider space where broken chairs and benches have been arranged. Some men and women sit here, most have painted faces and wear a variety of costumes. In the middle of this, the manager is reclining on an easy chair with the pipe of a hubble-bubble in his mouth, smoking tobacco with a serious face. Beside him an actor is sitting naked on the floor, wearing nothing but a pair of shorts. He is getting his beard shaved by the theatre's regular barber. This is where the manager holds his conference. In this gathering, conspiracies are being continuously hatched, people are reporting against each other, and flattering words are being spoken about the manager who presides over this gathering. There are very few places in Bengal as full of small-mindedness, meanness, and intrigue as the theatre. And it is astonishing to see how easily and for no reason, the creatures of this world can make a travesty of truth.

Nur Jahan returned from the stage her face full of annoyance and said, 'Today's audience is very bad. Only creating trouble, didn't clap for me.'

Miss Kiran was sitting on a bench with a spicy *kachuri* in her right hand, she was having it from a paper packet. She was more good-looking than Nur Jahan, and her utmost wish was to play Nur Jahan's role. But the manager's partiality had put paid to her hopes. Miss Kiran looked very pleased by the fact that Nur Jahan hadn't received any applause on stage that day. Now she began to snigger, hearing about Nur Jahan's disappointment and noticing her annoyed expression.

Outsiders are not aware about the extent to which the manager's writ runs over actors and actresses of the stage. Here, the manager's wish is as absolute as Napoleon's command. If he is happy then even the unworthy will get a role, and if he is annoyed then the worthiness of the truly worthy will be of no use. Managers often misuse their authority. I know one such retired manager—no actress could expect to secure a role without going to bed with him at least once. Who knows how many more such people are there in the world of theatre?

Perhaps Nur Jahan also adopted some such secret means to get this opportunity to appear before the audience. So she couldn't tolerate Miss Kiran's sniggering and stomped away furiously to the dressing room, sat down on a chair, and lit a cigarette.

Now, do you recognise that woman in the corner sitting before the mirror, about to paint her face? Don't shudder on seeing her complexion—black as the cuckoo, her balding head, her face pockmarked by pox, and her arms and legs thin like split bamboo, because she is Binodini, the 'ravishing songstress with the cuckoo's voice'. Babus and hordes of Marwaris of the city are salivating over the prospect of getting her address. Be a little patient and you will find how, thanks to the unparalleled glories of the dressing room, she has become beautiful like Tilottoma, the divine *apsara*.

Beauty in the world of theatre is always of this kind. Perfect beauty is surely not to be found here and in fact women of passable good looks don't remain here for long—it's impossible for them to do so. Whenever on those rare occasions, a beautiful woman makes her appearance on the theatre stage, inevitably a number of captains, who worship her beauty, emerge from the audience. And in a day or two this beautiful woman is not to be seen any more. On asking around it will be revealed that she is now bound up with such and such babu, and won't be acting in the theatre any more. And so, just like the sceneries, homes, houses, cities, costumes and furniture of the theatre-world, the beauty of the people here is also completely artificial, and they have no usefulness anywhere in the wide world except on stage. Therefore, I can vouch with certainty that those who harbour suspicions that Urvashi, Menoka, Rambha, and other beauties have really made their home in this so-called paradise, are completely mistaken.

A group of *sakhi*s dance as they pass through the wings on their way to the open stage. A man sits there, playing a harmonium. As each woman passes, he cracks some bawdy joke in a low voice.

Jester Monababu stands between the other pair of wings, talking in low tones with a buxom beauty. Her name is Bonchakhuki. Monababu has his eyes on Bonchakhuki for a long time but Bonchakhuki refuses to acknowledge it. Luckily for Monababu, having bagged Bonchakhuki's husband's role in today's play, has drawn her aside, trying to convince her that the relationship forged between them today should continue for all times.

'Oh bother! Why me, don't they sell ropes and pitchers in the bazaar?' Bonchakhuki winked and said.

At another end a group of young men—most of them skinny and looking completely worthless—stood or sat around, secretly cracking jokes and bantering with some *sakhi*s, discussing whether the manager had an eye for them or not. These *sakhi*s, who would be earning five to fifteen rupees, quite resembled these men. These are the apprentices. They don't get a salary and most of them don't hope to get any. They appear on stage as members of silent crowds or in the role of dead soldiers in battlefields—they are complete illiterates. Despite not getting any regular salary, these creatures are happy with the forbidden right to banter secretly with the *sakhi*s. However, the situation of these young men here is quite miserable because even the humble lizards of this place don't miss a chance to bluster and bully them with glaring red eyes.

After looking at this behind-the-scenes picture of the playhouse that we just presented, are you still suffering from the illusion that this is paradise?

Outside, the audience of the playhouse, tired from screaming and clamouring, had fallen silent. On the stage, Nur Jahan, Jahangir and the courtiers appear and leave time and again, but no one protests or shows any enthusiasm. The noses of certain members of the audience, while they continue to remain seated, transform into musical instruments. The nodding heads of a couple of sleeping members of the audience fall upon the shoulders of the next person. The more the annoyed person moves away, the closer the sleeping man's head slides, and falls upon him again…. Only the pit and gallery audience are still not completely disheartened. With every appearance of the *sakhi*s they become voluble and restless. When the main actors and actresses fail to entertain, what recourse is there but for the audience to whistle, clap and comment to cheer up the gathering? The grand 'success' that we read about, in advertisements of the Bengali theatre, is not achieved because of actors and actresses. It is bred in the dark depths of the gallery. Theatre's Goddess of Fortune resides in the galleries where there is no nuisance of 'free passes'.

ENDNOTES

1   **annotated** *Hootum Pyanchar Naksha* this book is published in Bangla, has extensive footnotes and an illuminating introduction by Arun Nag. See, *Satik Hootum Pyanchar Naksha* (annotated *Hootum Pyanchar Naksha*), edited by Arun Nag (Ananda Publishers, 2018).

2   **Hootum** is the author Kaliprasanna Sinha who wrote *The Observant Owl: Hootum's Vignettes of Nineteenth-century Calcutta* (Permanent Black, 2008), originally published in Bangla as *Hootum Pyanchar Naksha* (1862).

3   **renaissance** here the reference is to Bengal Renaissance, a flowering of creativity and intellectual growth in the fields of science, literature and the arts alongside religious and social reformist movements, which happened in Bengal (centred around Calcutta) and included figures like Rabindranath Tagore, Ram Mohun Roy, Jagadish Chandra Bose and many others. The period of Bengal Renaissance roughly stretches from late 18th century to the middle of the 20th century. See *Awakening-The Story of the Bengal Renaissance* by Subrata Dasgupta (Random House India, 2010) and *British Orientalism and the Bengal Renaissance: The Dynamics of Indian Modernization, 1773–1835* by D Kopf (University of California Press, 1969).

4   **Mandhata** an ancient mythical king. To say something is from Mandhata's times (*Mandhatar amol, literally the reign of Mandhata*) means it's from very long ago.

5   **Marwari** people originally from Rajasthan in India. A very successful business community, there have been many moneylenders and merchants among Marwaris and they settled in places like Calcutta. The reference to Marwaris is oft-repeated in this book.

6   **Naga mendicants** 'Sanyasi(s)' in the original are Hindu religious mendicants or ascetics. The Naga sanyasis are a subgroup of sanyasis who usually remain naked.

7   **kantha** a thin cushion made by stitching together old saris used instead of a mattress or bed. A *kantha* can also be used like a blanket.

8   **Satyendranath Dutta** (1882–1922) was a well-known Bengali poet of this period.

9   **Pir(s)** literally 'elder', is a Sufi master and spiritual guide.

10   **Vaikunthapur** or Vaikuntha is the celestial abode of Vishnu. *MaraterVaikuntapure* means a Vaikuntha on earth, that is heaven on earth.

11   **Chitteswari** a temple of Goddess Chitteswari (a manifestation of Durga) near the northern end of Chitpur Road, which is one of the oldest temples of Calcutta. The Chitteswari temple is variously associated with the name of the original founder Chite Dakat, a dacoit who went by the name Chite, as well as with that of Mahabir Ghosh who rebuilt (1610) the temple in the current spot.

12   **Kalikadebi** is the goddess Kali whose temple is located in Kalighat. The present temple structure is about 200 years old though the temple is mentioned in many earlier sources.

13   **on a tiger rides ...** '*byaghrobahini*' in the original is a Hindu goddess whose mount is the *byaghro* or tiger.

14 **tiger's den** refers to the swampy and riverine mangrove forests of the Sunderbans, the lair of the Royal Bengal tiger, which extended from the Gangetic delta in the extreme south of Bengal, up north to the region which is now Kolkata.

15 **saheb** a white European man. In certain contexts a white British citizen. In those times the boss at office would often be a white man and so the word 'saheb' has also come to mean the boss, which is a usage current to this day.

16 **Abu Hussain(s)** Abu Hussain here means an upstart, a parvenu. The name is used sarcastically to describe the lifestyles of babus. It comes from the title of a play by the distinguished actor-director-writer Girish Chandra Ghosh (1844-1912). The play is titled *Abu Hussain* or *Hotath Badshah*. *Hotath* means sudden and *badshah* is an emperor. Also see *hotath-babu*.

17 **palki-gari** literally a palanquin (*palki*) cart (*gari*). *Palki-gari* was an innovation of Brownlow, a British palki-maker and merchant who attached wheels to a palanquin and got it pulled by a single horse. Palki-garis became popular and were also called 'brownberry' after Brownlow. Samiparna Samanta citing Jitendranath Ray writes, 'Following the success of Brownlow horse-cart, Calcutta soon witnessed a plethora of European and indigenous hired horse-carts—Greenfield, Fiton, Bruham, Lando, Victoria, Bayrush, Gig, Keranchi, Chenkra, Chariot, Juri, TomTom, Ikka, Tanga— all flooded the streets of Calcutta.' Also spelled phaeton, landau and brougham. See *Banglar Kalkarkhana o Karigari Bidhyar Itihaash* by Jitendranath Ray (Dey's Publishing, 2005) and 'Cruelty Contested: The British, Bengalis, and Animals in Colonial Bengal, 1850-1920', a dissertation by Samiparna Samanta.

18 **barn-owls of Laxmi** the owl is goddess Laxmi's mount. Here the allusion is towards the nocturnal nature of these people.

19 **pipistrelle-bat** '*chamchike*' in Bangla, this is the Indian pipistrelle bat.

20 **ten-anna-six-anna hairstyle** the old Indian rupee consisted of sixteen annas. A ten-anna-six-anna hairstyle was a style of cutting the hair where ten parts is kept in the front and six at the back, basically long hair at the front and shorter at the back.

21 **hothat-babu** someone who has suddenly (*hotath*) become a babu, a parvenu; nouveau riche.

22 **Garher Maath** literally the fields (*maath*) around the fort (*garh*). Fort William of Calcutta is surrounded by wide open fields (esplanade) called Garher Maath. No construction was allowed in this area by the British to keep a clear line-of-fire for their cannons against invading armies. Garher Maath remains free of permanent constructions to this day.

23 **MLC** Member of the Legislative Council.

24 **non-cooperator** one who is a part of the Non-Cooperation movement (1920-1922) which was started by M.K. Gandhi against British rule following the Jallianwalla Bagh massacre.

25 **Brahmo** see Brahmoism below.

26 **swarthy boy from the milkman's quarters** is an allusion to the Krishna legend. Krishna (the lover) was dark and grew up among milkmen.

27 **Savitri** is a character from the Mahabharata whose story of bringing her husband Satyavan back to life from the clutches of Yama—God of death, earned her the title 'Sati' which means devoted.

29 **memsahib(s)** or 'mem' is a white European woman. A white European man is saheb/sahib. In certain contexts sahib and memsahib would indicate white British men and women respectively.

30 **peoples** often in this book the Bangla word *jati* (translated to 'peoples') is used to mean races, religions, ethnicites all taken together or separately any of these categories. *Jati* while literally meaning race, tribe etc. covers ethnic, religious, racial and other such categories in this book. This is because of a certain kind of usage still prevalent among some Bangla speakers where 'jati' covers different categories besides race and so usages like '*Hindu jati*' or '*jatey tara Musulman*' etc.

31 **second to none in India** the Goondas Act was promulgated in 1923 to control the goondas and their criminal acts as defined by the ruling British power.

32 **honoured in the goonda community** Ahmed Din was one such criminal operating from the Mechhobazaar area in the early decades of the last century which is the period the book refers too. Debraj Bhattacharya's paper about the Calcutta 'underworld' of this period says, Ahmed Din 'was the most influential man amongst the criminals and smugglers of Mechuabazaar where his name was held in awe'. This description seems to echo Meghnad Gupta's description. See *Kolkata' Underworld' in the Early 20th Century* by Debraj Bhattacharya (Economic and Political Weekly, Sept 18, 2004).

33 **gambling den** Debraj Bhattacharya writes that gambling dens were not owned by any particular community and that 'Chinese, the Peshwaris, the Anglo-Indians, the Marwaris and the Bengalis' have been mentioned in this context. However he also points out that opium smuggling in the 1920s was primarily in the hands of Peshwari Pathans and Chinese. *Ibid.*

34 **strip pedestrians** Debraj Bhattacharya in his categorisation of criminal activity in the early decades of the last century mentions this crime saying 'category consisted of men who intimidated the passers-by and snatched their valuables, threatening them with a knife, or may be even commit a murder.' He mentions Sugan Khan a beedi-maker as belonging to this category. See *Kolkata 'Underworld' in the Early 20th Century* by Debraj Bhattacharya (Economic and Political Weekly, Sept 18, 2004).

35 **Chinatown** the Chinatown described in this chapter is the 'old' Chinatown of Calcutta in and around Tiretta Bazaar. For a short history of the Chinese community of Calcutta see chapter 'The Chinese in South Asia' by Zhang Xing and Tansen Sen in the *Routledge Handbook of the Chinese Diaspora* edited by Tan Chee-Beng (2013).

36 **Tansen** (1500-1586) was a popular north Indian (Hindustani) classical music exponent.

37 **Jhuribhaja** Called *bhujiya* in the rest of India these are a savoury mix of thin strips of spicy, deep-fried gram flour sticks. Here the author seems to be having a variety of noodles for the first time in his life, which he compares to *jhuribhaja*.

38 **sikka** old Indian currency units. Four annas equaled 1 sikka and 16 annas equaled one rupee.

39 **anna** old Indian currency units. Four annas equaled 1 sikka and 16 annas equaled one rupee (taka in Bangla).

40 **Mogs** are people who originally came from the Arakan region of Myanmar (Burma) bordering the Bay of Bengal. The Arakan region currently falls in Rakhine state.

41 **gambling** (Chinatown) According to certain accounts, the game popular in Chinese gambling dens of Calcutta during or after the Second World War was mahjong. However at the time this book was written and from the description of the scene, it seems these people were playing fan-tan. For descriptions of gambling and opium dens of Calcutta's Chinatown see 'Lure of Chinatown' in *Crime and Religious Beliefs in India* by Augustus Somerville (1930). For an account of gambling, crime and drug addiction in Calcutta's Chinatown see *Kolkatar China Sampradayer Itihaas* (1871–2001) by Arpita Bose available at http://shodhganga.inflibnet.ac.in/bitstream/10603/50365/1/phd%20thisis%20of%20arpita%20bose.pdf (Accessed 18ᵗʰ February, 2019).

42 **patita** literally a fallen woman, a prostitute.

43 **bibi** is the feminine of babu (in this case the client) and here she is the prostitute.

44 **Karna** is an important character from the Mahabharata epic who was a selfless and generous ruler. Obviously there is a hint of sarcasm in the text about the apparent generosity of the babus.

45 **baya** one of the two drums of the tabla. The left hand drum is called baya and the right hand one the tabla.

46 **Basuki** is Shiva's serpent, a figure of Hindu mythology. He allowed the *devata*s and the *asura*s to twine him around mount Mandara and use him as a churning rope to churn the ocean of milk. This is why he is said to be tolerant.

47 **Tilottoma** a woman of incomparable beauty. The reference is to the celestial nymph, Tilottoma of Hindu mythology.

48 **upstart captain-babu** 'captain-babu' is an upstart, immoral, profligate and wasteful kind of babu who had an affinity for the British and had flourished under British rule in Bengal. An early mention of 'captain-babu' is found in Kalicharan Mitra's play 'Captain-babu' published in Calcutta in 1889. A character in Utpal Dutta's well-known play *'Tiner Talwar'* is also called captain-babu.

49 **Kashi Mitra ghat** another burning-ghat north of Nimtala.

50 *Bolo Hari Hari Bol*. A funeral chant of Hindu corpse bearers in Bengal.

51 **Samsan bhalobasish…hridi** this is a devotional song written by the Shakta poet-saint Ramprasad Sen.

52 **sakher-babu** in the original Bangla is a sub-class of babus given to a fanciful profligate life of merry-making.

53 **Star Theatre** recently renovated theatre hall near Hatibagan in north Calcutta. It is now primarily a cinema hall. From the location of Star Theatre and Beadon Street it's obvious that both Minerva restaurant and Minerva Grill were hotels located in Bengali neighbourhoods. These two establishments should not be confused with Minerva Hotel which is in Ganesh Chandra Avenue in central Calcutta.

54 **bearer** in this case bearer (*beyara* in Bangla) means someone who waits tables and serves food.

55 **Chine-Chameli** literally Chinese Chameli,where *chameli* is the name of a sweetly fragrant flower. Here it's the name of a prostitute which is why the analogy of the flower is provided soon after.

56 **Brahmoism** a theistic, reformist movement within Hinduism. Founded in Calcutta by Raja Rammohun Roy in 1828. According to Encyclopaedia Britannica, 'The

Brahmo Samaj does not accept the authority of the Vedas, has no faith in avatars (incarnations), and does not insist on belief in karma (causal effects of past deeds) or samsara (the process of death and rebirth). It discards Hindu rituals and adopts some Christian practices in its worship. Influenced by Islam and Christianity, it denounces polytheism, image worship, and the caste system.'

57   **Mawd** popular word for booze in Bangla.

58   **Matal Hari** this name used by the author literally translates to Drunken (*matal*) Hari. It also alludes to the famous Mata Hari, and the author surely had her name in his mind. Mata Hari (1876-1917) was an exotic dancer and courtesan who was convicted of being a German spy during the First World War and later had to face the firing squad.

59   **guli** an intoxicant, most probably small balls of *bhang*-which is an edible portion of the cannabis plant.

60   **big room** actually a large cabin with a number of tables. The 'hotels' described in this section are actually restaurants with many rooms or cabins of different sizes.

61   **Muhurram is for the Muslims** here a strange comparison is being made between the festival of a city and that of a particular religious community. Perhaps Calcutta being a somewhat Hindu majority city, the author is really subconsciously comparing a Hindu and a Muslim festival.

62   **dhaak** a kind of large drum played with sticks whose beats are associated with the Durga Pujo festival.

63   **dhol** a large barrel shaped drum, typically with two faces, originally used in South Asia.

64   **nahabat** musical performance comprising *sehnai* and other instruments.This recital is popular during marriage ceremonies and other festive occasions. The place where such performance is held is also called *nahabat*.

65   **siddhi** an intoxicant made from marijuana plant and consumed during festivals and otherwise. Known as bhang in other parts of India.

66   **alta** a liquid dye of lac, especially used by some married Hindu women to paint the borders of their feet.

67   **surma** a kind of dark eyeliner made from sulphate of antimony.

68   **subarnabanik** a mercantile group from Bengal involved in gold and silver trade. According to Jogendra Nath Bhattacharya (1896) their spiritual guides are the Chaitanite Gossains. See *Hindu Castes and Sects: An Exposition of the Origin of the Hindu Caste System and the Bearing of the Sects Towards Each Other and Towards Other Religious Systems* (digital ed.). by Jogendra Nath Bhattacharya (Thacker, Spink.). https://archive.org/stream/hinducastesands00bhatgoog/ hinducastesands00bhatgoog_djvu.txt (Retrieved 28 January, 2019)

69   **Phooldol** a Hindu festival associated with Dol (eastern India) and Holi (rest of the country). This is one of the spring festivals where flowers ('*Phool*' means flower and '*Dol*' is a swing) are important and it leads on to Holi. Fulera-duj celebrated in other parts of the country is similar to Phooldol in Bengal. There are various traditions in Hinduism linking Holi with Krishna, Vishnu, Siva and other deities but the strongest association of Phooldol is with Radha and Krishna's divine romance.

70   **capital city** it can be assumed that this chapter refers to a time before 1911, when Calcutta was still the capital of British ruled India.

71   **Vidyasagar** full name Ishwar Chandra Vidyasagar (1820–1891) was a Bengali educator, writer and social reformer who brought major changes to society by campaigning for remarriage of widows, opposing child marriage, and fighting other ills.

72   **Golapi beedi** a kind of beedi. Beedi is a cheap, thin Indian cigar where tobacco leaf is used instead of paper.

73   **kartal** a percussion instrument used in devotional and other music.

74   **beggars' quarter** a fictionalised account about a beggars' group and life at a beggars' quarter of Calcutta can be found in *Pataldangar Panchali* by Juvanaswa (Century Press, 1956).

75   **Manu Samhita** traditionally the most authoritative of the books of the Hindu code in India which lays down dharma for the Hindus.

76   **literary outpourings** see **beggars' quarters** above for an example of a mid-century literary work about beggars of Calcutta.

77   **puriya** a wrapper containing small measure of a drug like cocaine.

78   **adda** here adda means a den or place from where drugs are sold.

79   **Bankimchandra** Bankim Chandra Chattopadhyay (1838–1894), noted Bengali author.

80   **bhang** an intoxicant made from the marijuana plant.

81   **Bidyasundar's Malini** Malini is a flower-girl character from the play *Bidyasundar* (based on a poem of the same title) about the love story of princess Bidya and prince Sundar. The Bidyasundar performance mentioned in the book was definitely based on poet Bharatchandra Ray's (1712–1760) poem of the same name which was part of his larger work *Annada Mangal*.

82   **swadeshi** meaning domestic, something homegrown and belonging to one's own country. The reference is also linked to the Swadeshi movement which was part of the Indian independence movement. The Swadeshi movement was launched after the first Partition of Bengal (1905) and was aimed at self-reliance and hurting British power by boycotting foreign products and promoting the revival of domestic products, culture and production processes.

83   **English theatre** here and elsewhere means proscenium style European (usually meaning English) theatre. The word used in the original is *bilet* which can mean English and European both but in the context of theatre and playhouses of Calcutta of those times, it means English. For a detailed background of Bengali and European theatre of this period, see *Bangla Theatre er Itihaas* by Darshan Choudhury (Pustak Bipani, 1995) and for a snapshot view, see, 'Stage, Society and Stricture: Bengali Theatre, 1800–1876' (2013–14, Vol. 2, *Vidyasagar University Journal of History*).

84   **khemtaa** a kind of folk dance accompanying *khemtaa* songs. It is performed by women or eunuchs. Here is a description of such a *khemtaa* performance, 'The *khemtaa* nautch began. The *khemtaa* wallas sang a saucy song from behind, while two middle-aged *khemtaa wallis* danced rhythmically, swaying their hips to the song. After some time, the *khemtaa wallis* went up to the guests and stretched out their hands like poor Brahmins to collect tips. The nautch ended at two o' clock

in the night. The *khemtaa* wallis began to frequent the rooms of the patrons, the puja ground was sanctified.' This description of *khemtaa* is from *The Observant Owl: Hootum's Vignettes of Nineteenth-century Calcutta*, by Kaliprasanna Sinha; translated by Swarup Roy (Permanent Black, 2008).

85 **Bengali theatre** theatres run by Bengalis as described earlier in this chapter.

86 **from Barobazaar** the implication here is about poor taste and lack of finesse as Barobazaar (Burrabazaar) is a commercial district of Calcutta and it's being assumed by the author that the people from that area don't possess finer tastes.

87 **Hatkhola** an area near Nimtala burning ghat. The implication here is about unrefined tastes of the people of this area.

88 **Notun Bazaar** a bazaar of that name off Chitpur Road near Pathuria Ghat street (Pathureghat in this book). Also spelt Natun Bazaar.

89 **Hatha yoga** a system of yoga involving among other things difficult contortions and postures.

90 **Kropp razor** a brand of razor made in Sheffield England during this time. The trademark 'Kropp' was used by Osborne, Garrett & Co. from 1899 to 1923.

91 **Nur Jahan and Sher Khan** Nur Jahan (1577–1645) born Mehr-un-Nissa was the twentieth wife of Mughal Emperor Jehangir. She was earlier married to Sher Afgan Khan (Sher Khan) who was governor of Bihar. The love story of Nur Jahan and Jehangir has been fictionalised with embellishments and unsupported plotlines in movies, poetry and other media.

92 **Sheoratola** is any place where Sheora (*Streblus asper*) tree(s) grow. Sheora trees are supposed to be haunts of *petni(s)* which are ugly-looking female ghosts. So the comment among other things draws attention to the woman's ugliness by saying she lives in Sheoratola.

93 **captains** same as captain-babu. See the entry for **upstart captain-babu**.

94 **bound up with** and *bandha* (tied) in the original Bangla have a similar meaning in this context. Means the woman is not free to see anyone she pleases but is tied or fettered to a particular babu. Bound (from Anglo-French *bounde* from Medieval Latin *bodina*) in English is cognate with *bandhan* in Sanskrit (*bandhan* in Bangla).

95 **ropes and pitchers** basically asking him to drown himself by tying a pitcher round his neck.

ACKNOWLEDGEMENTS

Despite claiming to be a die-hard Calcutta addict somehow I hadn't come across Meghnad Gupta's *Raater Kolkata* till very recently. So I must first thank my friend economist Brati Shankar Chakraborty who mentioned the book and piqued my curiosity by narrating the episode of the escape from the goonda's den. I am indebted to Arunava Sinha, who is an inspiration for translators, for facilitating the permission and generally for his suggestions. Louise Ardenfelt Ravnild, another translator friend, also enriched my work with some valuable suggestions about the nuances of the translator's art. Hemendra Kumar Roy's granddaughter Sudeshna Chakraborti not only helped this project by providing the necessary permission to translate this work but, also being an English teacher herself, provided useful feedback. I am grateful for her enthusiasm. The book being from another time, there are several words, turns of phrase and references which were not always clear on first reading. In navigating through meanings, connotations, usages and certain historical references, I have been assisted by friends, historians and language experts among whom I must mention Arpan Chakraborty from the Bengali Department of Maulana Azad College, Sudeshna Dutta who teaches English and my friends Priyadarshi Basu, Niharul Islam and Agni Roy. As always, my wife Anuradha had been my first reader and critic.